CW01639252

This study on rural development and restructuring is part of t
Regional Development's (ICLRD) ongoing initiative to support
approaches to cross-border and inter-jurisdictional spatial pla
development through joined-up analysis and research. Funding from the Irish Government, through the Higher Education Authority (HEA), has supported this work programme which brings together a multi-disciplinary research team drawn from five academic and research organisations on the island of Ireland and the United States.

Acknowledgements

The ICLRD would like to thank the Advisory and Steering Committees for their assistance, advice and guidance throughout the duration of this research. We also convey our sincerest thanks to the numerous interviewees and focus group attendees who were consulted during the course of this study; the views and opinions expressed contributed significantly to this work.

The research team further take this opportunity to thank the ICLRD partners for their support during this study and both Justin Gleeson & Pamela Dore of the All-Island Research Observatory (AIRO) for their assistance in the mapping of various datasets.

Advisory Committee

- Mr. Niall Cussen, Department of the Environment, Heritage & Local Government
- Mr. Paul Donnelly, Department of Agriculture and Rural Development
- Mr. Padraig Maguire, Border Regional Authority
- Ms. Susan Scally, Department of Community, Rural & Gaeltacht Affairs[1]
- Mr. Mike Thompson & Mr. Jim Hetherington, Department for Regional Development

Steering Committee

- Mr. Michael Doyle, IRD Duhallow
- Mr. Brian Murray, Workspace, Draperstown
- Fr. Sean Nolan, Truagh Development Association

Research Team

- Ms. Caroline Creamer, NIRSA, NUI Maynooth
- Dr. Neale Blair, University of Ulster
- Dr. Karen Keaveney, Queens University Belfast
- Dr. Brendan O'Keeffe, Mary Immaculate College, University of Limerick
- Mr. John Driscoll, Institute for International Urban Development

Maps by Justin Gleeson & Pamela Dore, All Island Research Observatory (www.airo.ie)©
Photos courtesy of the NIRSA Photo Archive (www.photoarchive.ie)© and ICLRD (www.iclrd.org)©

HEA

Higher Education Authority
An tÚdarás um Ard-Oideachas

1. Replaced by Ms. Dairearca Ni Neill and Mr. Micheal O'Corcora in February 2009.

About the Authors

Caroline Creamer is a Research Fellow with the National Institute for Regional and Spatial Analysis (NIRSA) at the National University of Ireland, Maynooth. She is also an associate researcher with the International Centre for Local and Regional Development. Her research interests include regional and local development and regeneration, spatial planning, and inter-territorial and cross-border development.

Dr. Neale Blair is a lecturer with the School of the Built Environment, University of Ulster and an associate researcher with the International Centre for Local and Regional Development. He is a chartered town planner, and is active in research projects commissioned by local government and research councils to examine issues relating to, inter alia, public participation and brownfield development in Europe.

Dr. Karen Keaveney is a Lecturer in the School of Planning, Architecture and Civil Engineering in Queen's University Belfast. Karen is an affiliate of the Joint Centre for Housing Studies, Harvard University and the International Centre for Local and Regional Development. Her research interests include the spatial literacy needs of planners, cross-jurisdictional planning, rural restructuring and individual and community perceptions of space and place.

Dr. Brendan O'Keeffe is a lecturer with the Department of Geography, Mary Immaculate College, Limerick and an associate of both NIRSA and the International Centre for Local and Regional Development. His research interests include territorial governance, rural development and sustainability; to date, he has carried out research and project evaluation work for the EU as well as local authorities and voluntary organisations in the community development sector.

John Driscoll is Director of the International Centre for Local and Regional Development and Vice President of the Institute for International Urban Development, Cambridge, Massachusetts. He has over 30 years experience of cross-regional planning, urban regeneration and economic development in the United States, the EU, Central and Eastern Europe, the Middle East, Sub-Saharan Africa and Asia.

The information and opinions expressed in this document have been compiled by the authors from sources believed to be reliable and in good faith. However, no representation or warranty, express or implied, is made to their accuracy, completeness or correctness. All opinions contained in this document constitute the authors judgement as of the date of publication and are subject to change without notice.

This document is intended to provide general information on the subject matter of this publication. It is not intended to provide a comprehensive statement of the subject matter and does not necessarily reflect the views of the constituent partners of ICLRD. Unless otherwise agreed, no other party may copy, reproduce, distribute or make use of the contents of this publication.

Table of Contents

GKZ 3578

BACKGROUND

Contemporary planning policy, both urban- and rural-focused, is largely directed from the European level; its main objectives including long-term sustainability, increased competitiveness and balanced growth. Contestations arise, however (and somewhat inevitably) when member states begin to translate these policies into national, regional and local government strategies and actions. This is largely because these policies, as devised by the European Union, cannot take account of the individuality of place and space.

Rural areas throughout Europe have evolved in different ways over the past half century, resulting in there being many types of 'rural' – ranging from the very remote to the peri-urban – as well as functional diversity. Each type of rural area experiences its own range of challenges, some of which are generic and others which are place-specific. Rural development and diversification, together with economic regeneration, has been ongoing across the island of Ireland since the onset of the 'rural crisis' in the late 1970s and early 1980s. Initial schemes, however, tended to focus on the disadvantages and inequalities of the rural and resulted in their being regarded as a 'liability'. More recently, there has been a shift in emphasis, with the focus now being placed on the potentiality of the rural. At the same time, agriculture continues to play an important role in rural development and environmental management; and it is likely that, as a result of the current global economic change and growing interest in the 'local food movement', there will be a growth in the numbers 'returning to the land' over the medium-term. The economic climate is also generating increased pressures for further rural diversification that is centred on local asset-bases and which is geared towards the harnessing of this endogenous potentiality – without being over-reliant on external funding or other interventions.

This research programme builds on previous research carried out by the International Centre for Local and Regional Development (ICLRD); namely:

(a) *Fostering Mutual Benefits in Cross-Border Areas: The Challenges and Opportunities in Connecting Irish Border Towns and Villages* (Creamer *et al*, 2008)
(b) *Spatial Strategies on the Island of Ireland: Development of a Framework for Collaborative Action* (Inter*Trade*Ireland, 2006)
(c) The discussions as part of the ICLRD's annual conference in January 2008 during which the need for greater emphasis to be placed on the needs of rural communities, in terms of their future development, was highlighted.

These, together with other studies and policy documents (see **Chapters 1** and **2**), demonstrate that there is a growing recognition that rural areas – and their balanced development – are an important policy area in their own right; and that the current political climate facilitates the development of rural communities on a North, South and cross-border basis.

For the past twelve months, the ICLRD (see Appendix 1) has been considering the role of rural restructuring and economic diversification, together with the growing importance of the rural-urban relationship, in the achievement of balanced spatial development across the island of Ireland. While a number of communities have been successful in restructuring their economies, others have been less so. Through three case study areas, this research study reflects on what took place between the mid-1980s to present day when rural diversification was promoted as a method of regenerating rural economies and the solution to the 'rural crisis' throughout Europe. The three case study areas at the centre of this research programme are:

- Draperstown, Magherafelt District
- Emyvale-Truagh-Aughnacloy on the North Monaghan / South Tyrone border
- Duhallow, North West Cork / East Kerry (see Figure 1).

During this research programme, over 80 people were interviewed, either on a one-to-one basis or through the forum of focus groups (see Appendix 2) and detailed desk-based analysis, covering policy documents, academic literature and local and national media reports, was undertaken. A comprehensive Working Paper series was developed out of this action research phase and these can now be downloaded from the ICLRD website (see www.iclrd.org). In addition, a 1-day conference was held on 8th May 2009 at which 110 delegates representing a range of sectors (from local government officials and elected representatives to owners of micro-enterprises) further considered and debated the opportunities and challenges in adopting a holistic and local asset-based approach to rural development.

Both Draperstown and Duhallow have been engaged in the process of rural restructuring for the past twenty-five years and, over this time, have built up a wealth of experience; not only from their successes but also from initiatives that have not worked out and / or not gone to plan. For Emyvale-Truagh-Aughnacloy, the challenges facing this rural community are complex and it too has had its successes and failings. Historically, the challenges facing this cross-border community have been further exacerbated by its border location and the impact of decades of back-to-back policy development between both administrations on the island of Ireland.

More recently, the economic downturn has seen many initiatives and enterprises in the three areas struggle to survive and / or 'go to the wall'. What all three communities have in common, however, is their commitment to the development of their respective areas and, as they look to the future, questions which they have been asking of themselves and other stakeholders in the field of rural development include: Who has, and what is, the 'vision' for the rural? What role has local potential / assets to play in the process of rural restructuring? To what extent is there vertical and horizontal integration between policy and practice as it relates to rural development? and What role does education and life-long learning have to play in rural development? – questions that will resonate not only with rural communities throughout the island but also with local government officials and elected representatives, community and local development agencies, businesses and business networks, practitioners, policy-makers and academics who are engaged, directly and indirectly, in rural development and regeneration.

Figure 1: Location of Case Study Areas

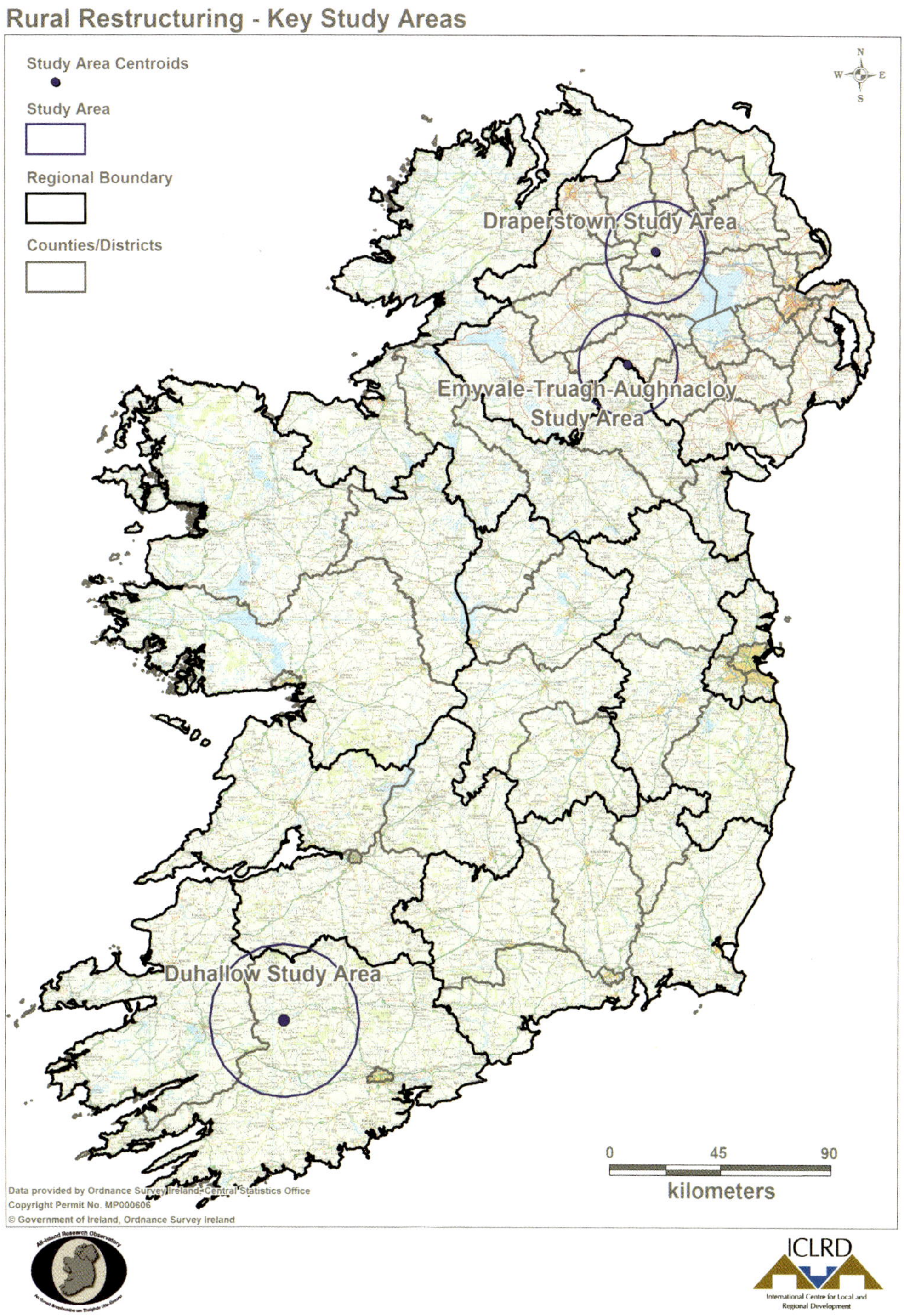

(Prepared by AIRO, 2009; © Ordnance Survey Ireland / Government of Ireland Copyright Permit No.MP000606)

FOREWORD

Mr. Peter Quinn
Businessman & Former President, GAA

Despite the huge growth in first-world prosperity, the massive expansion of new technologies, or the wonderful developments in original ideas and innovative applications, economic and social progress continues to travel a very uneven path. From the industrial revolution, which created unprecedented social unrest before delivering equally unprecedented prosperity, through the 'dot.com' revolution, with its bubble which burst creating major consequences for inventors, investors and employees, to the collapse of the Celtic Tiger, with its banking crisis, its negative equity, its adverse transformation of national finances and its rapid growth in unemployment, the 'two steps forward and one step backward' nature of economic and social change is reflected consistently.

Indirectly, this report from the International Centre for Local and Regional Development (ICLRD) supports that view of progress. The development of sustainable solutions to the problems of rural communities and their economies in Ireland is challenging; their implementation will be even more challenging, largely because there are too many fingers in 'this pie' – from EU directives, to national and local planning policies, to bureaucratic governance structures and, ultimately, to the absence of a coherent vision for rural society. An integrated approach will be essential, if we are to make progress, in this area.

Rural Ireland is blessed with strong communities, which function as supports for their members and which provide powerful bases for economic development. Such development never occurs in a vacuum; it needs a social and cultural framework within which to flourish and rural communities in this country provide those pre-requisites – the people (in most cases, people with both skills and commitment), the sense of identity, and the sense of togetherness and of co-operation which is essential in the establishment and growth of economic entities. In terms of facilitating factors, those are huge, but frequently unrecognised, strengths. There are also the role models of significant, rurally-based, economic successes. And we have the interest in enterprise and industry, which are inherent elements of farming communities; in the past, that was best demonstrated through the co-operatives, but it also existed where there were no such organisations. The old tradition of the 'meitheal' is still alive in rural Ireland; even if its status has reduced from what it once was.

Across the island of Ireland, we continue to have opportunities. Recession or no recession, there are still people with ideas for both on-farm and off-farm diversification – people with ideas in relation to both incubation and innovation. Many, probably most, of them need help. In most cases, that help involves money and capital can still be sourced for good projects - especially if those with the ideas are prepared to share with those with the capital. It can be a slow, torturous process to get a business up and running, but think of how the co-operatives developed in another era when there was less wealth and fewer enterprises.

I have a strong view that every area, defined broadly, possibly as broadly as a whole county, or part of a county – or the micro-region, as advocated in this study – should have a group, which meets three or four times a year (or maybe less) to explore the possibility of establishing new businesses, to identify what would encourage people to start their own businesses, to examine the impediments which those with ideas feel exist and to consider how such impediments could be overcome. I am confident that if people had access to good, experienced, mentoring support, either provided on a voluntary basis or subsidised by an existing support agency, we would see the establishment of many more new businesses in rural Ireland. A major impediment to starting a new business is the risk and uncertainty involved, the fear of failure and the danger of losing what one already has or owns. A good mentoring programme would go a long way to reducing those fears and it should be considered.

To those of us who have our roots in rural Ireland, the final four conclusions from this study of 'real life' experiences are both sensible and consoling in their logical simplicity. They place a greater emphasis on product than on process, the importance of celebrating success instead of deriding failure (as we are so prone to do on this Island), the need to invest in people and the absolute necessity to re-invest in communities. When taken in tandem with the acknowledgement that not all such initiatives will succeed – that risk applies to community activity and to rural development projects just as it does to other forms of investment and that, if we seek progress, we must tolerate risk and failure too – these conclusions, however basic they may first appear, are the fundamental building blocks for any programme of rural restructuring or community development.

There is more – much more – to this study, but those simple conclusions justify the time and money involved. They should no longer be mere conclusions – they should become the starting points for future community and rural development policies. And, for the benefit of decision-makers and funders, they should be 'writ large' as the fundamental tenets of such policies.

June 2009.

PART 1:
Setting the Context

© IRD Duhallow

CHAPTER 1:

Rural Restructuring in Context

Key Messages

- Uneven development and the recognition that the rural is comprised of differentiated spaces are amongst the greatest challenges to establishing an effective vision for the future of the countryside.

- Although faced with declining traditional economic bases in recent decades, rural areas are well-positioned to adapt to changing demands given the traditional reliance on small-scale businesses.

> *"The world we have created today as a result of our thinking thus far has problems which can not be solved by thinking the way we thought when we created them".*
>
> **(Albert Einstein)**

- The growth in employment sectors such as construction and manufacturing in small to medium sized towns throughout the island of Ireland highlights the influence – and subsequent vulnerability – of rural populations to dramatic shifts in local and global economies. In the current economic climate, the long-term sustainability of such industries, as a core economic base in the countryside, is rapidly contracting.

- The legacy of laissez-faire rural interventions, together with the complex policy environment and disconnected nature of traditional 'trend' planning, is a significant barrier to the sustainable spatial development of the rural.

- In terms of strategic spatial planning, both horizontally and vertically, there is a lack of institutional fit and strategic orientation across agencies on the island of Ireland. Yet, collaborative spatial planning has an important role to play in addressing and meeting the needs – social and economic – of both rural and urban communities on the island.

Changes that have occurred in rural areas across the island of Ireland over recent decades have had profound effects on how the countryside functions, on its role and on the demographic profile of those living outside urban areas. The traditional distinction between rural and urban areas has gradually evolved as a result of increased spatial mobility and the need for rural dwellers to regularly travel to towns and cities to access employment and services. This, in turn, has resulted in the repositioning of long-established urban and rural dichotomies and in fluctuating ideas about the future role of the countryside. Uneven development and the recognition that the rural is comprised of differentiated spaces are among the greatest challenges to establishing an effective vision for the future of the countryside; this, in response, points to the need to effectively and strategically plan for the new rural(s).

Prior to planning for the rural(s), it is important to first define what the rural is and the different types that may exist. A number of definitions have been developed for the island of Ireland and by the European Union (EU) and the Organisation for Economic Cooperation and Development (OECD) for the wider global region (see, for example, CSO, 2006a; NISRA, 2005; Callanan *et al*, 2004; McHugh, 2001; OECD, 1994); with the greatest challenge for conclusive rural definitions being the identification of where the urban ends and rural begins. While all definitions recognise that rural areas range from peri-urban, high density populations to remote, dispersed populations, it must be remembered that villages and towns exist across these scales. Therefore, in order to adopt a workable definition of the rural for this study, rural areas are defined as areas that have a density of less than 150 persons per square kilometre (OECD, 1994). This definition is compatible with the combined functional definitions of both the Irish Central Statistics Office (CSO) and the Northern Ireland Statistics and Research Agency (NISRA) which identify areas with a population ranging from 1000 to 2000 as rural / open countryside[2]; with the implication that the closer to the maximum the more peri-urban the settlement becomes.

The rural must be acknowledged as integral to regional and national balanced development. This is particularly significant as we move into the uncertain global economic period ahead and are faced with changing public funding mechanisms and structures. While the emerging multi-functionality of rural areas provides major challenges for balanced development going forward, it also presents a number of opportunities to respond in unique ways to global economic restructuring at the local level. These include opportunities in food consumption, recreation, energy production, ICT, social enterprise, nature conservation and emerging models of collaborative local governance.

Although faced with declining traditional economic bases in recent decades, rural areas may in fact be well-positioned to adapt to changing demands given the traditional reliance on small-scale businesses (be it farming or light industry, for example). This requires, however, national frameworks to be in place to support diversification; ensuring that communities can respond to challenges, and progress and evolve in the most appropriate way.

1.1 Rural Restructuring on the island of Ireland

The 1980s was a period of the 'farm or rural crisis' in Western Europe. Agriculture and other primary and associated activities, long considered the cornerstone of the

2. The 2005 NISRA report, *Report of the Inter-Departmental Urban-Rural Definition Group – Statistical Classification and Delineation of Settlements,* establishes areas and settlements with a population of less than 4,500 persons as the default definition for 'rural' (Bands F, G and H). For the purpose of this study, Band F – Intermediate settlements – are constituted as peri-urban and therefore not included in the definition of 'rural' adopted.

rural, came under increased pressure. There was an undermining of the productivist (intensive) representation[3] of the rural. This was brought about by over-production and 'trade wars' in external export markets. The social composition of rural areas also began to change; improvements in accessibility and mobility, for example, allowed more urban workers to live in the countryside. A number of factors drove the transition of agriculture and wider rural change, including a growth in rural tourism and recreation; rising rates of car ownership; second home ownership and / or retirement to the countryside; large-scale industrial development in rural areas; and counterurbanisation where the countryside began to be viewed as a desirable place to live (Clout, 1998).

On the island of Ireland rural areas, particularly those areas not located in close proximity to large urban centres, have also been experiencing a wide range of challenges since the early 1980s. This rural crisis included a decline in agriculture, the loss of services, a 'brain-drain' and out-migration; all of which raised questions about the future viability of small and peripheral rural settlements. The Border area on the island of Ireland is presented with additional and particular challenges for the future of its rural economies and society. As a result of the 'border effect' and the ensuing Troubles, the area has suffered from decades of back-to-back policy development, lack of inward investment and the decline of its communities – socially, economically and physically. It is increasingly recognised that the reversal of this downward spiral can only be achieved through inter-sectoral, inter-institutional and inter-jurisdictional cooperation and collaboration. Just as the rural must be integral to any strategy for balanced development, the themes of cross-border cooperation, regional competitiveness and rural restructuring are inextricably linked.

1.2 Economic Change

In the Republic of Ireland there was a 40% decline (60,228 persons) in the number of people working in agriculture from 1991 to 2002, falling by another 8,000 people by 2006 (CSO, 2006b). At the same time there were increases in other employment sectors, particularly in the construction sector. The picture for Northern Ireland (in the 2001 Census) is very similar, where only 3% of the population were recorded as working in farming compared with 14% employed in construction industries. This steep decline in agricultural employment reflects a period across the island of Ireland and beyond where the productivist countryside has changed to become more complex and is increasingly determined by external consumer and changing internal demands. In addition, the growth in employment sectors such as construction and manufacturing (seen in industries such as furniture making and joinery) in small to medium sized towns throughout the island, highlights the vulnerability of rural populations to dramatic shifts in local and global economies.

Rural economic diversification has occurred as a result of direct and indirect state and EU intervention and subsidisation both of agriculture and of other rural economic activities and services, together with changing consumer demands and internal and external markers. This has resulted in progressive increases in on- and off-farm employment. EU initiatives such as LEADER have been to the fore in supporting rural

3. The productivist era, which spanned the post-World War Two period up to the 1970s and 1980s, involved rural areas undergoing an industrialisation of agricultural practices. This included intensified production, greater mechanisation, output specialisation and concentration, and reliance on the state protection of prices (Woods, 2005).

enterprise development. Small-scale light industries that grew interdependently, for example, have expanded beyond the farm gate becoming involved in, for example, the construction sector. The challenge now is that sectors such as construction and manufacturing are under renewed pressure and their long-term sustainability as a core economic base in the countryside is rapidly contracting. The global economic change and how it is being played out at the state level only serves to stress that if already vulnerable communities move from over-reliance on one sector to another they are leaving themselves open to economic and societal weakening. Therefore, further diversification is required in most rural areas, particularly those that are located at some distance from major urban settlements and outside commuter belts.

1.3 The Rural Dweller

The ongoing desire to live in the countryside that is apparent throughout the island of Ireland brings both positive and negative potential. A vibrant and active community on the one hand can result in pro-active strategies for diversification; while on the other hand, the need to sustain a relatively large population on a limited economic and infrastructural base poses a number of difficulties. The changing relationship between rural and urban places, and the processes that are at work in shaping the contemporary countryside, are reflected in demographic and socio-economic characteristics. These include incremental depopulation and repopulation, changing household structures, and increased mobility and accessibility beyond rural areas. Since the industrial revolution rural populations in Western Europe have been in flux, with mass movement from the countryside to towns and cities characteristic of this era when employment and the desire for a better quality of life drew people into urban areas (Pacione, 1984). Long-term rural depopulation ensued resulting in a strengthening and consolidation of urban areas. However, improved mobility and accessibility from the mid-twentieth century onwards resulted in a widespread reversal of rural depopulation trends.

On the island of Ireland a weak urban fabric with low population densities, coupled with the maintenance of relatively high rural populations despite emigration, means that counterurbanisation may not be as significant a feature of urban-rural movement as in other Western countries. The foundation for what remains a sizable rural population base is largely a result of the relatively late emergence of an urban-industrial society throughout the island, which for the Republic of Ireland only began to emerge in the 1960s (Bartley, 2007). High levels of access to land due to farm-family ownership, together with the ease with which planning permission can be obtained to construct new dwellings in the countryside – particularly in the Republic – and the spatial and environmental factors that impact on housing costs, has meant that living in rural areas has always been a viable and common alternative to living in urban centres. In addition, socio-cultural factors such as agricultural change, while undoubtedly impacting on

... further diversification is required in most rural areas, particularly those that are located at some distance from major urban settlements and outside commuter belts.

population movements to peri-urban and urban areas in search of employment, have also opened up land for development. The end result is a relatively high proportion of the national populations continually living in rural areas and a largely consistent level of low concentration / density development. However, as illustrated in the island of Ireland census atlas (Gleeson *et al*, 2008) these trends have manifested themselves differently across the island with two principle characteristics apparent: (a) an east-west divide in terms of higher population densities and growth being found in the greater Dublin and Belfast areas, leading to peripherality in much of the West, South-west and Midlands; and (b) remoteness and peripherality in the Irish Border region due to inaccessibility and a legacy of back-to-back policy.

1.4 The Rural Community

Achieving sustainable rural communities is an important objective in both rural development and spatial planning, and although this creates a significant challenge for agencies either side of the Border and across the island, it is one which has been reiterated by a number of visions and policies over a long period (see **Chapter 2**). Within rural society, however, a number of vulnerable groups are identifiable that require particular attention and who need specific support from the wider community and from public bodies in particular. For example, groups such as migrants, youth and older dependent people are more likely to need significant supports and structures. Smallholder households are particularly vulnerable given the reduction in off-farm employment and this has the potential to lead to financial problems and a greater likelihood of isolation for those living in single person households. A further challenge facing many rural communities is gender inequity – not only in terms of employment but also in governance, education, health and risk of poverty (Northern Ireland Assembly, 2002).

Interestingly for the island of Ireland, the dispersed rural community advocated by the Rural Development White Paper (1999) for Ireland and the *Regional Development Strategy* (2001) for Northern Ireland, although presenting challenges for environmental sustainability, may in the context of the wider rural Europe provide an alternative model of rural development into the future. With the current uncertainty regarding global and national economies, rural areas may, as mentioned above, be in a strong position to adapt to local economic changes given their tradition of small-scale, flexible businesses.

1.5 The Rural Land and Landscape

Land, sea, landscapes and seascapes represent significant resources for rural development. To date, these have been viewed and utilised as spaces of production, with some of the more scenic rural areas having a parallel recreational function. The values associated with 'the land' on the island of Ireland hinge on notions of sense of place, attachment to home, and the expectation that as a land owner one has the right to develop that land as one sees fit.

In more recent times this has manifested itself in contestation about how land should be used and who has the right to decide how it is used. An example of this contestation includes the highly evocative rural housing debates that have occurred in both Ireland and Northern Ireland[4]. In addition, concerns have been voiced that rural activity is too 'EU-led' and that the farming community is not engaging enough with the wider rural development debate (PricewaterhouseCoopers, 2005). As a result, rural land has become a contested space where debates about the future of the countryside are played out.

1.6 Rural Development and Spatial Planning

From the 1950s onwards, spatial planning has been characterised by a need to instigate anticipatory planning rather than being "… characterised by ad hoc solutions and timing dictated by crisis" (Graham, 1976:xii-xiii; cited in Lapping, 2006:113). This new era viewed land-use planning as an integral part of national economies and a number of countries at the time began to implement systematic policies, such as the identification of hierarchies of settlement for the attraction of different levels of foreign direct investment (FDI). However, with the increasing emphasis of planning on urban areas and the continued integration of rural and agricultural policy, rural planning had, and continues to have, unclear goals. In the case of Northern Ireland (and the wider U.K.) this resulted in the adoption of intermittent restrictive policy and highly regulated planning in the countryside for development other than that which is agriculture-related.

The legacy of laissez-faire rural interventions (which is more prominent in the Republic of Ireland), together with the complex policy environment and disconnected nature of traditional 'trend' planning, is a significant barrier to sustainable spatial development. This is because the capacity to deliver growth is hindered by the stop-start approach to relationship building between stakeholders; the uncertainty that occurs when responsibilities are continuously shifted or re-organised within government agencies; and also the fragility of funding streams to which community organisations are susceptible. Understanding the operation of rural development agencies and policy influences is problematic as the structures and organisational boundaries can often appear to be impermeable.

…there is a lack of institutional fit and strategic orientation across agencies on either side of the Border.

The issues described above are compounded in the Irish context by the Border. Take for example the case study area of Emyvale-Truagh-Aughnacloy (see Figure 1). The local layer of government incorporates Monaghan County Council and Dungannon and South Tyrone Borough Council, each with an economic development strategy. On top of this layer come the various support agencies for rural enterprise development. In the South, these include the County Enterprise Boards, County Development Boards and LEADER groups at a local level and Enterprise Ireland and Industrial Development Authority (IDA) Ireland at a regional level. In Northern Ireland, support agencies include local enterprise agencies and LEADER groups at the local level, and Invest NI at a regional level. Other support agencies, with no financial element, include FAS (the national training and employment authority),

4. This includes, for example, *Draft Public Policy Statement (PPS) 21: Sustainable Development in the Countryside* in Northern Ireland (and its predecessor, Draft PPS14) and the *Sustainable Rural Housing Guidelines* in the Republic (2005).

Business Innovation Centres (BICs) and Area Partnerships in Ireland and Area Partnerships in Northern Ireland. Further layers of spatial planning also exist through area / county plans and the *National Spatial Strategy* (NSS) for Ireland and *Regional Development Strategy* (RDS) for Northern Ireland respectively. Taken together, these demonstrate that there is a lack of institutional fit and strategic orientation across agencies on either side of the Border. Moreover, the layers of enterprise agencies tend to cause confusion at local level, and this concern is compounded by their perceived rigidity and distance from the needs of entrepreneurs and rural communities.

As a process, collaborative spatial planning has an important role to play in addressing and meeting the needs of both rural and urban communities on the island of Ireland. However, both jurisdictions are still engaged in the process of preparing and rolling-out traditional land-use focused county and area / district plans. With the exception of the all-island non-statutory collaboration framework currently being finalised by both governments, the process and focus of collaborative spatial planning is still at a very early stage in its development on the island of Ireland. Divergent systems, North and South of the Border (i.e. a localised planning administration in the Republic of Ireland and a centralised system in Northern Ireland), pose particular challenges for collaborative, inter-jurisdictional planning.

To be successful, the process of rural development necessitates stakeholders engaging in the process of strategic spatial planning; where the economic diversification, social process and environmental conservation involves cross-border development and collaborative spatial planning. Collaborative planning is one means of turning these local challenges to opportunities and meeting the objectives of Lisbon, Göteborg, the European Territorial Cooperation Agenda and the wider Rural Development Programme (see **Chapter 2**); and at a more local level, the aims and objectives of Ireland's NSS and Northern Ireland's RDS. This process will involve:

- Developing a vision
- Focusing on people as well as space
- Working in partnership with a wide range of stakeholders
- Promoting capacity building within the communities themselves and among agencies
- Delivering better governance.

© IRD Duhallow

CHAPTER 2:

A Collage of Visions

Key Messages

- Rural areas are highly complex, non-homogeneous places; the development of which is increasingly associated with inter-county and intra-regional connectivity and an evolving relationship with neighbouring urban centres and regions.

- Visions for how the rural should develop have largely tended to emanate from the European Commission and filter into national (and thereafter regional and county-level) policy. Largely sectorally-focused, these various strategies and frameworks have promoted the development of rural economies through diversification that is both innovative and creative in its drive and end-goals.

> *"... there is no longer one single rural space, but rather a multiplicity of social spaces that overlap the same geographical area".*
>
> **(Cloke and Milbourne, 1992:360)**

- There is increasing recognition of the need to address the territory rather than specific sectors; and that each area requires a tailored approach to meet its local challenges. A territorial approach to development will decrease regional disparities by addressing the wider needs of rural areas and lead to economic dynamism including entrepreneurial and innovative actions.

- Despite policy advances towards integrated rural development, the EU reforms of the Common Agricultural Policy (CAP), while naming 'rural development' as a pillar, have not heretofore been accompanied by a sufficient re-direction of resources away from productivism and on-farm based activities towards wider rural development.

- **More still needs to be done in terms of acknowledging rural development as a policy area in its own right while at the same time, shifting emphasis away from the traditional urban / rural dichotomy. The current review of the *Regional Development Strategy* (RDS) for Northern Ireland, together with the 'refresh' of the *National Spatial Strategy* (NSS) and the review of the *Regional Planning Guidelines* for Ireland, generates opportunities for putting in place a strategic and structured framework that promotes the rural-urban relationship through the adoption of a local asset-based approach to balanced development.**

In line with the increasing acknowledgement that there are many types of rural area – ranging from the weak and marginalised to the peri-urban (McHugh, 2001) – there is a growing volume of literature produced by a myriad of commentators outlining various 'vision(s)' for rural development. These 'visions' take many forms, cover a broad range of issues, exist across varying spatial scales, are applied at various geographical levels and fall under the remit of a wide range of institutions, from the supra-national to local level. While these visions have the potential to be helpful to rural communities in the most generic sense, the challenge lies in their broadness but also in their being *aspatial* – that is, having no relationship to the locality in which they may eventually be applied. Also, while the noted visions may give guidance in terms of the 'what' and the '*where*', little is recorded on the '*how*' or the '*who*'.

The end result has, therefore, been a frequent disconnect between the visions emerging at an EU, national, regional and county level and their application at a local or 'micro' level – and in many instances, an uncertainty in what actually constitutes a 'vision'.

2.1 Existing Vision(s) for the Rural

Rural areas are increasingly (and rightly) regarded as highly complex, non-homogeneous places; the development of which is increasingly associated with inter-county and intra-regional connectivity and an evolving relationship with neighbouring urban centres and regions. To this, one could also add the growing economic pressures resulting from globalisation versus the needs of the local – and the implications of both on rural development. Policy for growth and development has a responsibility not only to adjust to these changes, but to adopt a proactive approach to transformations in the rural economy rather than maintaining the status quo of reactive responses. Both European agricultural policy and regional investment policy, for example, have over past decades had wide impacts on the scale and nature of rural economies. Yet, from its establishment in 1958 to the early 1990s, rural policy within the European Union was largely (and narrowly) concerned with agriculture; an emphasis that resulted in a somewhat tapered view of, and stunted framework for, rural development. Similarly, rural policy on the island of Ireland was largely concerned with agriculture until recent decades. It was only when farming and traditional countryside economies began their explicit decline in the late 1970s and early 1980s (the 'rural crisis' as discussed in **Chapter 1**) that the parameters of rural policy were widened to include (a) broader rural development programmes and (b) the future of communities – other than farming – living outside areas of growing urbanisation.

With this broadening of the definition of what constitutes rural development, there has been a raft of publications and strategies over the past two decades which make reference to the future growth and development of rural areas – physically, economically, socially and culturally. These 'visions' have mostly tended to emanate from the European Commission and filter into national (and thereafter regional and county-level) policy. Largely sectorally-focused, these various strategies and frameworks have promoted the development of rural economies through diversification that is both innovative and creative in its drive and end-goals – thus leading to job creation and increasing competitiveness – and which, over the long-term, leads to sustainable growth.

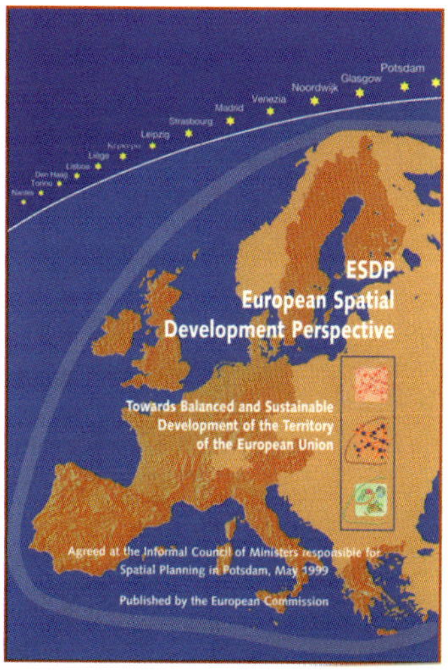

Prior to the publication of the *European Spatial Development Perspective* (ESDP) in 1999 – a landmark document in terms of a shift to thinking spatially rather than sectorally on development policy – *The Future of Rural Society (*CEC, 1988), the White Paper on Growth, *Competitiveness and Employment: The challenges and ways forward into the 21st Century* (CEC, 1993) and *Europe 2000+* (CEC, 1994) outlined the role of the countryside within the European territory; presenting the rural as having an important function within the urban realm as a buffer between centres, being an area for recreation and tourism, and as supporting new populations through the development of their own economies through the promotion of small and medium sized enterprises (SMEs). A clearer integrated vision for rural development emanated through the *Cork Declaration*, published in November 1996 under the Irish presidency of the EU (and further elaborated on by the *Salzburg Declaration* in 2003). This 10-point proposal for integrated rural development policy called for, among other things, greater coherence across sectoral policies as they relate to sustainable rural development; that policy must be multi-disciplinary in concept and multi-sectoral in application; and all policy must have a territorial dimension.

In this same period, the MacSharry Common Agricultural Policy (CAP) Reforms in 1992 attempted to change the direction of farming from what was unsustainable production to the consolidation of quotas. It also entailed the incentivisation of farmers to engage in alternative and complementary economic activities, including the pursuit of a role as guardians of the countryside. Changes in agricultural policy continued throughout the 1990s; for example through *Agenda 2000* (CEC, 1997) and the decoupling of farming output and income support in the mid-term review of the CAP in 2003. These reforms provided for an EU-wide framework for rural development policy taking into account the changing nature of the rural population and the need to look beyond agriculture as the main activity and source of income in the countryside. Economy, culture, location, social and environmental factors and population density (and the differences within them) were now recognised as contributing to the experience of people living in these areas and to patterns of settlement and development.

The aforementioned ESDP, published in 1999, recognises the new and emerging challenges facing rural areas such as, on the one hand, the changing viability of traditional agricultural practices sometimes located in peripheral areas with poor infrastructure and accessibility and, in contrast, places that are experiencing growing pressure from their location close to urban centres. The "… treatment of the city and countryside as a functional, spatial entity with diverse relationships and interdependencies" and the recognition that in "… a polycentric urban system the small and medium-sized towns and their inter-dependencies form important hubs and links, especially in rural areas" (CEC, 1999: 24) are of particular importance for the development of rural areas of all types.

There is increasing recognition of the need to address the territory rather than specific sectors; and that each area requires a tailored approach to meet its local challenges.

It was also at this time that a specific document for the future of the countryside was adopted by the Irish Government in the form of the White Paper for Rural Development: *Ensuring the Future - A Strategy for Rural Development in Ireland* (Department of Agriculture and Food, 1999). This paper called for the rural proofing of all government policies and frameworks so that the countryside would be treated as another element of the national economy and society – and not as a separate entity reliant on agriculture alone. It also encouraged a vibrant, dispersed settlement pattern and community. To date, no such document has been adopted for Northern Ireland; although proposals for a Rural White Paper for Northern Ireland were agreed by the Northern Ireland Executive in April 2008 and is currently being progressed by the Department for Agriculture and Rural Development (DARD). When finalised, it is envisioned that this White Paper will set out the Executive's collective commitment to rural development.

At the turn of the Millennium, increasing emphasis was placed on sustainable growth and economic competitiveness at an EU, and subsequently national, level. For example, the *Lisbon and Göteborg Strategies*, adopted in 2000 and 2001 respectively, prioritise the goals of growth, competitiveness and job creation, and sustainability respectively. Building on this, the *Community strategic guidelines for rural development* and associated *Rural Development Programme* for the period 2007-2013 have, as one of their objectives, the improvement of quality of life in rural areas and diversification of the rural economy (CEC, 2006a). There is increasing recognition of the need to address the territory rather than specific sectors; and that each area requires a tailored approach to meet its local challenges. A key goal of the new rural development programme, under which each member state must prepare a broad framework of action, is to turn the challenges facing rural areas into opportunities by developing local infrastructure and human capital which in turn will improve conditions for growth. To this end, Axis 3 – Quality of Life – measures under the Rural Development Programme for Northern Ireland are being delivered through Local Action Groups (LAGs) that are comprised of local councillors and social partners and which are supported by the District and Borough Councils. The councils, organised in clusters, have developed rural strategies for their respective areas and funding has been allocated based on this spatial / territorial approach.

On a cross border basis, the *European Territorial Cooperation Agenda*, also covering the period 2007-2013, promotes cooperation through a partnership of national, regional and local agencies in the areas of:

- SME development
- Tourism
- Environmental protection
- Health care

- Infrastructural development
- Greater accessibility to information and transport networks
- Education, cultural and linguistic development.

Such territorial cooperation, it is argued, will decrease regional disparities by addressing the wider needs of cross-border rural areas and lead to economic dynamism including entrepreneurial and innovative actions.

The common link between these policy guidance documents and programmes for action is the recognition that rural areas offer potential for growth – through amenities, service delivery and natural resources – which remains largely untapped. The growth and development of rural communities, however, is dependent on the nurturing of the rural-urban relationships, creation of economies of scale, building up the *necessary* critical mass, ensuring value-added and taking cognisance of the uniqueness of each rural community.

2.1.1 A 'Vision' Disconnect?

The EU has been responsible for the introduction of the area-based / territorial approach to rural development that has become a feature of rural governance. EU declarations, such as the aforementioned Cork and Salzburg Declarations express commitments to a *Living Countryside*, multi-functionality, partnership governance and spatial differentiation. Despite these advances towards integrated rural development, the EU reforms of the Common Agricultural Policy (through *Agenda 2000* for example), while naming 'rural development' as a pillar of the CAP, have not heretofore been accompanied by a sufficient re-direction of resources towards wider rural development and away from productivism and on-farm based activities (ESPON, 2004; Commins, 2004). The relative under-resourcing of LEADER, for example, at EU and national levels can be attributed in large part to the lobbying power of farm organisations which have convinced successive administrations that funding should continue to accrue to on-farm activities – to the exclusion of activities in the broader rural economy.

2.1.2 A Changing Policy Landscape

For the most part current policy has managed to recognise that the rural comprises of differentiated, heterogeneous spaces and places; but in reality has not formulated or applied a differentiated, heterogeneous response. The spatial strategies for Northern Ireland and the Republic of Ireland – the RDS and NSS respectively – made significant progress in recognising the complexity of rural areas by placing, for example, emphasis on dynamic rural-urban relationships and linkages. However, while recognition is one thing, a proactive response is another. The lack of a comprehensive strategy for the open countryside and the adoption of relatively ambiguous rural policies has, over the past decade, placed both spatial strategies somewhat uncomfortably alongside the objectives set out in the aforementioned *The Future of Rural Society, Europe 2000+* and the *European Spatial Development Perspective* (ESDP). In many ways, the NSS and RDS comply with the requirements of these frameworks; for instance, by recognising differentiation across space and the non-homogeneity of the countryside. However, rather than adopting a complex differentiated policy to address the emerging complexity of rural space, the 'ambiguous approach' has, to date, been presented as a positive – leaving the responsibility of negotiating contestation to the local level. But without a distinctive framework in which local government can adopt rural strategies, achieving rural sustainability remains a challenge.

However, the current review of the *Regional Development Strategy* for Northern Ireland, together with the 'refresh' of the *National Spatial Strategy* and the review of the *Regional Planning Guidelines* for Ireland generates opportunities for putting in place a strategic and structured framework and promoting the adoption of a local asset-based approach to rural restructuring and diversification.

2.2 Who is Implementing these Visions?

Contemporary rural planning policy is now largely directed from the European level, based on objectives for long-term sustainability, and implemented at the regional and local levels. The problem that lies at the centre of rural development policy and associated spatial planning is the uncertain future of the countryside in light of ongoing urbanisation, increased reliance on knowledge-based economies and the continual need for high quality and efficient food production. The Irish Border adds an additional, challenging layer of need and expectation through the tradition of a relatively large rural population; an ongoing desire to live in the countryside in a wealthy, rapidly urbanising society; and the presence of the Border itself. While the RDS for Northern Ireland, and to a greater extend the NSS for Ireland, provide some clarification on the roles and potential of rural spaces and communities, institutional, governance and policy vacuums persist, particularly at regional and sub-regional levels.

Since the 1970s, and particularly since Ireland and the U.K. joined the European Union in 1973, the rural agenda has widened with a number of agencies such as Teagasc (the Irish Agriculture and Food Development Authority) and the National Economic and Social Council (NESC) in the South, and the Rural Development Council (RDC) and Rural Community Network (RCN) in the North making significant contributions to national and regional policy for the countryside. In addition, both governments have initiated a number of programmes and schemes in rural areas in order to assist in future social and economic sustainability, such as CLÁR (Ceantair Laga Árd-Riachtanais / Programme for Revitalising Rural Areas) in the Republic of Ireland and the Environment and Countryside project funding in Northern Ireland. Activities that address rural poverty and social exclusion are also being promoted at departmental level. The importance of the countryside to national government in both the Republic of Ireland and Northern Ireland was reiterated in 2002 at Ministerial level – albeit in different ways. In the Republic, rural affairs was separated from agriculture with the establishment of the Department of Community, Rural and Gaeltacht Affairs; while in the North, the brief

... without a distinctive framework in which local government can adopt rural strategies, achieving rural sustainability remains a challenge.

of the Department of Agriculture for Northern Ireland (DANI) was widened to include rural development and this is reflected in the Department's new name, the Department of Agriculture and Rural Development (DARD).

2.3 Reconciling the Visions

Much more still needs to be done in terms of acknowledging rural development as a policy area in its own right while at the same time, shifting emphasis away from the traditional urban / rural dichotomy. An ongoing challenge for rural policy and spatial planning on the island of Ireland is that no policy document exists that comprehensively addresses planning in the countryside. While sectoral policies including those for housing, water quality, and provision of services have been published for Ireland, responsibility for the countryside and its associated needs across this range of sectors rests with a number of government departments including the Department of the Environment, Heritage and Local Government, Department of Community, Rural and Gaeltacht Affairs and the Department of Agriculture, Fisheries and Food. Likewise in Northern Ireland, rural development and planning are the functions of three separate government departments; namely Department of Agriculture and Rural Development, Department of the Environment and Department for Regional Development; with the breakdown of responsibility including the Department of Environment being in charge of operational planning matters while the Department for Regional Development oversees strategic functions.

But what of the role of local communities in visioning? Should a vision not be something in which they are not only actively engaged in implementing but also in determining its focus in the first instance? – rather than being something that is imposed by central and regional administrations?

In the context of Northern Ireland for example, there are a number of opportunities currently available to improve community engagement in the visioning process. A key objective of DARD's *Rural Strategy 2007-2013* is to define and develop the rural champion concept (DARD, 2006). This will include the adoption of a joined-up approach to rural development policy across government, the development of an evidence-base that identifies rural needs and a reinvigorating of rural proofing. The rural champion concept has been subject to public consultation and final proposals are currently with the DARD Minister for consideration. In addition, the ongoing Review of Public Administration (RPA) in Northern Ireland, whereby the number of district councils will be reduced from twenty-six to eleven, presents opportunities in terms of community planning and visioning. With two years left to complete the preparation process for this major transition in governance structures (i.e. 2011), key elements of the change include:

- The introduction of a community planning process
- The transfer of a range of functions including aspects of planning, rural development, the public realm aspects of local roads, urban regeneration, housing related functions and local economic development and tourism
- The transfer of some 1,100 staff and £116m of expenditure from central to local government (Department of Environment, 2009).

Effective community development – irrespective of whether it takes place in rural or urban communities – is dependent on local stakeholders having a shared vision on how the community should develop to the benefit of all local actors (achieved through negotiation); being aware of local endogenous assets and their development potential (not only the 'how' but also the 'who'); recognising the value of rural / urban alliances; and committing to local capacity building over the medium- to long-term. It is these key aspects of rural development 'visioning' that have been absent for the most part in the preparation and roll-out of past – and present – strategies. And it is to these areas – principally the role of community, rural-urban relationships and local endogenous potential – that greater efforts and resources must be committed going forward in the development and implementation of rural community 'visions'.

PART 2:
Unleashing the Potential

9936
Ulsterbus
Bus Stop
Aughnacloy
Timetables made easy:
Call 028 90 66 66 30 or click www.translink.co.uk
73
76

CHAPTER 3:

Partnership – Integrating Top-Down and Bottom-Up

Key Messages:

- Tacit knowledge or local expertise is very important to the success of partnerships; communities know why things happen a certain way. Therefore, spaces must be created whereby local experts can come together to address indigenous issues – and when relevant, this should include local government.

- In terms of capacity building, a system is needed whereby a key role of the community development worker is to impart the knowledge and skills for maintaining the partnership to the wider committee; thus reducing the risk of the partnership 'folding' when the funding ends or the community worker leaves.

"...enduring competitive advantages in a global economy lie increasingly in local things – knowledge, relationships, motivation – that distant rivals cannot match".

(Michael Porter, 1998)

- Given the institutional arrangements in both jurisdictions on the island of Ireland, the onus of *enabling* area-based development lies with central government and the regional authorities in the South and the Northern Ireland Executive in the North (top-down) while local agents, ranging from council officials to community development officers and volunteers, are responsible for identifying the nature of, and facilitating and carrying out such development (bottom-up).

- Networks of smaller towns can play a significant role particularly within peripheral and remote rural areas, in enabling them to generate critical mass, and thereby sustain and anchor public services and businesses.

- **Gaining comparative advantage in a territorially cohesive area involves identifying the capability of that locality. This is based on the approach of networking, establishing inter-territorial relationships and recognising what an area can do rather than what it cannot.**

During this research, important recurring questions were 'what is a partnership?' and 'who should be involved'? Partnerships tend to be local; but there is a growing sense that they need to be wider than this – both geographically and in terms of membership. It is increasingly understood that partnerships do not take shape automatically; rather it takes time to build a partnership and it requires freedom of movement – for individuals to 'try it out' and walk away if it is not right for them. Furthermore, when engaging in a partnership, it is important that the 'partners' realise this is not now about them and their needs; instead, it is about the wider community and its needs.

The term 'community economy' describes the interplay of three integral elements that comprise a local socio-economy: public service, private enterprise and the third sector / volunteers (Pearse, 2003). This model is highly applicable to rural development and restructuring where that interplay of sectors and partnership of actors must be achieved in a balanced manner in order to realise future sustainability.

Through community development in rural areas, voluntary bottom-up action provides the potential to pro-actively plan for the local economy, better understand local needs and address area-specific challenges. Tacit knowledge or local expertise is very important to the success of partnerships; communities know why things happen a certain way. Spaces must be created whereby local experts can come together to address indigenous issues. At the same time, the need for a strong, focused and relevant top-down framework within which such local development can operate sustainably is paramount.

3.1 Partnership for Sustainable Rural Development

It is essential for sustainable growth and development that communities, businesses and local administrations work together on social, economic, environmental and cultural issues into the future. This cooperation is already taking place, as demonstrated by how the three case study areas in this research programme used the resources available to them to address their respective identified local needs (see Table 3.1).

While high levels of sectoral integration are observed at the local level throughout the island of Ireland, this is weaker in terms of top-down and cross-departmental integration and often lacks a spatial dimension. The approach that is necessary going forward is that partnership is secured both sectorally and spatially at all levels of governance. Central government support for area partnerships and businesses must be flexible and address local needs; with partnerships and businesses in turn having a territorial and multi-sectoral focus. Such a framework must be given a stronger position in the hierarchy of plans[5] and within formal government / governance structures (as described in **Chapter 1**). At the local level, this will necessitate stakeholders taking risks and stepping outside of their comfort zones – adopting an innovative 'can do' attitude rather than depending

5. For the Republic of Ireland, the hierarchy of plans includes the *National Spatial Strategy* (NSS), the *Regional Planning Guidelines* (for each of the eight regional authorities), County / City Development Plans and lastly, for those settlements over 1,500 persons, Local Area Plans. In Northern Ireland, the hierarchy consists of *the Regional Development Strategy* (RDS), District Area Plans and Local Area Plans.

Table 3.1: Territorial Resources in Draperstown, Emyvale-Truagh-Aughnacloy and Duhallow

Resources	Draperstown	Emyvale-Truagh-Aughnacloy	Duhallow
Human Resources	- Population decline of c.1% per year - High youth dependency.	- Population growth similar to all-Island average - Ageing population - In-migration of 'frontier workers.'	- Legacy of population decline - Disadvantaged by core-periphery approaches to planning.
Culture and Identity	- Plantation heritage with distinctive architecture - Musical tradition.	- Significant ecclesiastical structures - Strong agri-food sector - Communities overcoming back-to-back existences.	- Sliabh Luachra traditions well recognised - Emerging appreciation of ancient heritage features.
Physical Resources	- Designated Area of Outstanding Natural Beauty (AONB) - Scenic Landscape.	- Drumlin landscape with loughs and valleys - Some development pressures - River Blackwater – a cross border resource.	- Varied landscape - Proposed SAC and NHA[6] designations – need to be expedited due to development pressures.
Know How and Skills	- Low level of third level qualifications - Training provision locally by Workspace.	- Below average educational attainment - Brain Drain - Need for adult training and education.	- Below average educational attainment - Brain Drain - Need for adult training and education.
Economic Activities and Business Firms	- Below average unemployment in recent years - Entrepreneurship tradition - Dependence on manufacturing and construction.	- High level of dependence on agriculture - Heavy reliance on construction in Aughnacloy - Several small manufacturing businesses – flexible but under pressure.	- High level of dependence on agriculture - Reliance on manufacturing and construction in West - LEADER-supported job creation very significant.
Markets and External Relations	- Workspace a strong driver of connectivity, including cross-border collaboration.	- Strengthening cross-border linkages - Recognition of common / shared element of heritage - Participation in institutional cross-border networks.	- High level of participation in regional, national and EU networks - Inter-business collaborations.
Image and Perception	- Sense of isolation has strengthened identity and resolve for action - Emerging rural tourism sector.	- Emerging local branding - Commitment to the smart economy.	- Strong inter-community connections with high levels of social capital and clear territorial identity.

on others. In this regard, there are lessons that can be learned from the case study areas of Duhallow and Draperstown.

IRD Duhallow, together with Ballyhoura Development[7], are unique among Irish LEADER Partnerships in that their catchment territories transcend county / administrative boundaries. However, trans-boundary operations are common among LEADER Local Action Groups (LAGs) in other EU member states, and in some countries – such as Germany – they are encouraged as a means of fostering inter-municipal collaboration. The case study area of IRD Duhallow interfaces with both Cork and Kerry County

6. These proposed designations consist of Special Areas of Conservation (SACs) and Natural Heritage Areas (NHAs).
7. Ballyhoura Development operates in the South-west of Ireland on the borders of counties Tipperary, Limerick and Cork.

Councils on an on-going basis; and officials and elected members interface with one another mainly through the South West Regional Authority. However, it is only through the IRD Duhallow Board and Working Group meetings and associated events that councillors from East Kerry (Killarney Electoral Area) and North-west Cork (Kanturk Electoral Area) have an opportunity to meet one another in any formal capacity; that is, outside of political party meetings. Thus, IRD Duhallow is the only mechanism for cross-county collaboration between two electoral areas within a boundary of 30km. Such inter-county collaboration between local authority officials is very limited throughout the island, and there is little evidence of any collaboration in planning or the provision of infrastructure and amenities. Thus, in this respect, the situation in Cork / Kerry (inter-county) differs little from that which pertains between the border councils of, for example, Monaghan County Council and Dungannon and South Tyrone Borough Council (inter-jurisdictional).

Within the Draperstown area, there is a sense that statutory 'champions' of rural development are not yet fully effective. Evidence from the focus groups undertaken as part of this research programme indicates there is a perception amongst rural communities that government agencies have not effectively delivered on economic growth. In parallel with this, communities deem that government policy – and that of the support agencies – intimates that local initiatives are a 'hindrance' (rather than a help) and are, for the most part, unlikely to succeed. Workspace, however, proves any such perception wrong; as does other similar initiatives such as the Coalisland Development Association and the Newry & Mourne Cooperative Enterprises – organisations that were also established to address significant local needs in the absence of government intervention.

In terms of the sustainability of a partnership, capacity is becoming an issue – who has the capacity or receives the relevant training to establish, operationalise and lead a partnership that works towards sustainable rural development? Despite the investment by government, North and South, into capacity building over the past two decades and the large up-take of this training by community groups, it is arguable whether all existing networks and partnerships have the expertise and know-how to lead development. This is largely an issue of retaining trained staff; the community development worker, often the recipient of capacity training, will generally have to leave the organisation when the funding stream that covers the cost of their position ends; a scenario that is exacerbated by the time-lag between one funding programme ending and another beginning. Going forward, a system is needed whereby a key role of the community development worker will be to impart the 'learned' knowledge and skills necessary for maintaining the partnership to the wider committee; thus reducing the risk of the partnership 'folding' when the funding ends or the community worker leaves.

"... inter-county collaboration between local authority officials is very limited throughout the island, and there is little evidence of any collaboration in planning or the provision of infrastructure and amenities".

Utilising the expertise of existing champions, volunteers and groups (such as elected representatives and local authorities) to bring about meaningful partnership means investing in them: but also identifying that personnel are key to long-term sustainability. In particular, this may require national government to revisit the structures it recommends for area-based development groups under the 'Cohesion Process'. For example, the new governance structures for area partnerships including LEADER groups in the Republic of Ireland, whereby board members serve a maximum term of three years, creates a 'roving' board where long-term involvement is not encouraged. This raises doubts over the achievability of Cohesion's objective of: "to strengthen democratic accountability of agencies"; rather it is likely that a pontential legacy of expertise and experience may be lost.

3.2 Connecting Bottom-Up and Top-Down

Exclusively endogenous approaches (local and internal) to local development are unlikely to have sufficient resources to sustain themselves, particularly in the short- to medium-term; and in this respect, partnership between the bottom-up and top-down is essential. Partnership can only operate effectively if it exists within a connected framework that works from the bottom-up and the top-down. In effect, this means that the local must work with the national; that local agencies which have the greatest understanding of their catchment areas[8] need to work with supports from the regional and national level and within structures that are relevant and focused on local needs. From the three case study areas that are central to this research, it is evident that although the various organisations found it necessary to adopt a largely bottom-up approach given their circumstances and requirements at the time, all agreed that engagement from top-down structures is vital to the long-term sustainability of rural areas; and that key to the success of bottom-up / top-down integration is the horizontal engagement of agencies from local to national levels.

The state and its local agents have a key role to play in rural development, and need to be spatially-attuned and sensitive in the allocation of public resources. The OECD identifies four types of aid which public authorities can direct towards rural areas:

- Direct aid (to assist with increasing production capacity)
- Indirect aid (removing the barriers towards enterprise development)
- The enhancement of infrastructure
- Human resource development (OECD, 2005a, 2004).

Partnership can only operate effectively if it exists within a connected framework that works from the bottom-up and the top-down.

In terms of spatially differentiating between rural areas and the type of aid they receive, the OECD recommends that remote rural areas should focus on human resource development in tandem with infrastructure development; with direct aid being more applicable to intermediate rural areas. Drawing on international examples, the Organisation argues that the various forms of aid need to be integrated and delivered in a co-ordinated manner (OECD, 2005a, 2004). Given their largely endogenous roots and track record over three LEADER Programmes, Northern Ireland's – and in particular Ireland's – cohesive rural development partnerships offer an effective mechanism for aid delivery and co-ordination.

8. Gaining such an understanding is dependent of a wide range of local stakeholders working together – community development and resident associations, chambers of commerce or other such business networks, sporting organisations such as the GAA, dependency support agencies (Active Age, People with Disabilities), etc.

The pursuit of territorial approaches to rural development is optimised by the formation of collaborative governance structures that enable bottom-up participation and partnership between local actors and the state. While the bottom-up can play the lead role in identifying and articulating local priorities and can untap local knowledge, goodwill and social capital, the top-down has to assume the lead role in the provision of technical knowledge and financial resources, and in introducing a wider strategic vision that encompasses national objectives and targets and, where relevant, EU directives and guidance. The dispersal of increasingly limited European and national (public) resources needs to both reflect and promote a spatially differentiated approach, and in this respect policy makers are challenged to depart from traditional approaches that have tended to be spatially blind and to pursue new methods in line with the principles and objectives of the *European Spatial Development Perspective* (ESDP). Thus, given the institutional arrangements in both jurisdictions on the island of Ireland, the onus of *enabling* area-based development lies with central government and the regional authorities in the South and the Northern Ireland Executive in the North (top-down) while local agents, ranging from council officials to community development officers and volunteers are responsible for facilitating and carrying out such development (bottom-up).

3.3 The Changing Rural-Urban Relationship

Small and medium sized urban centres have a key contribution to make to balanced regional and territorial development. They can and do act as providers of services and drivers of sub-regional growth. Towns have the potential to attract inward investment into rural territories, and it is incumbent on local authorities to provide infrastructure and services in rural towns that not only meet current requirements, but also anticipate future needs, be that for growth and / or improved quality of life. Urban, rural and village renewal schemes, provided they are developed and delivered in consultation and partnership with local stakeholders, enhance the attractiveness of rural towns as places in which to live and work; schemes that are imposed from the top-down, and do not involve local citizens, have generally been unsuccessful.

Many market towns have experienced considerable changes over recent decades, as they have tended to lose customers and economic activities to larger urban centres. In response, ESDP advocates a polycentric approach, whereby towns collaborate with each other to develop specialised and complementary functions. At a national level, the importance of collaborative networks of urban settlements has been reiterated by the *National Spatial Strategy's* identification of 'A Hierarchy of Access to Social Infrastructure' which identifies sets of appropriate functions and services for settlements from the village scale upwards; acknowledging that small towns are an integral part of the rural economy and supporting the wider argument that settlements should not be considered in isolation from their wider locality (Courtney & Errington, 2000). At a local level, networks of smaller towns can play a significant role, particularly within peripheral and remote rural areas, in enabling them to generate critical mass (thus lessening the degree of isolation) and thereby sustain and anchor public services and businesses.

In order to manage a balance within the rural-urban relationship, it is important that planning authorities, in particular, engage with rural areas to understand local needs, identify the appropriate scale of ongoing development based on social, economic and environmental capacity, consider drivetime distances over particular timeframes (see Figures 3.1, 3.2, 3.3) and establish what role the village-town network can play in supporting its hinterlands – and vice versa. Understanding approximate drivetimes for example assists in visualising where rural-urban relationships do – and can – exist in terms of access to services and employment. An overriding objective for planning authorities is to ensure a good quality of life for all citizens – and drivetime isochrones are a useful tool in this respect. Within this objective, decisions regarding the provision and maintenance of services that are located in urban centres need to be assessed under criteria that include future population projections and demographic profile, and quality of life issues throughout the area.

3.4 The Principle of Comparative Advantage

The endogenous potential of local rural areas should be realised to achieve comparative advantage. Within this, local assets and existing 'countryside capital' (Garrod *et al*, 2006) are key to untapping this endogenous potential. Superficially, the idea of comparative advantage has a strictly economic meaning. However, when used within the context of rural diversification, it engages with all elements of territorial identity and long-term

sustainability (economy, society and environment). Gaining comparative advantage in a territorially cohesive area, that is an area that forms a micro-region (discussed in **Chapter 4**), involves identifying the capability of the locality. This is based on the approach of networking, establishing inter-territorial relationships, and recognising what an area can do rather than what it cannot. In effect, comparative advantage means: taking account of existing rural assets within a coherent territory; engaging partnerships within a bottom-up / top-down framework; integrating local (and national) agencies horizontally; and innovating, cooperating and competing within a regional, national and European context.

Figure 3.1: Drivetime Isochrones for Draperstown

Draperstown Study Area - Off Peak Approx Drivetime Isochrones: 0 - 10, 10 - 30, 30 - 60, 60 - 90 minutes

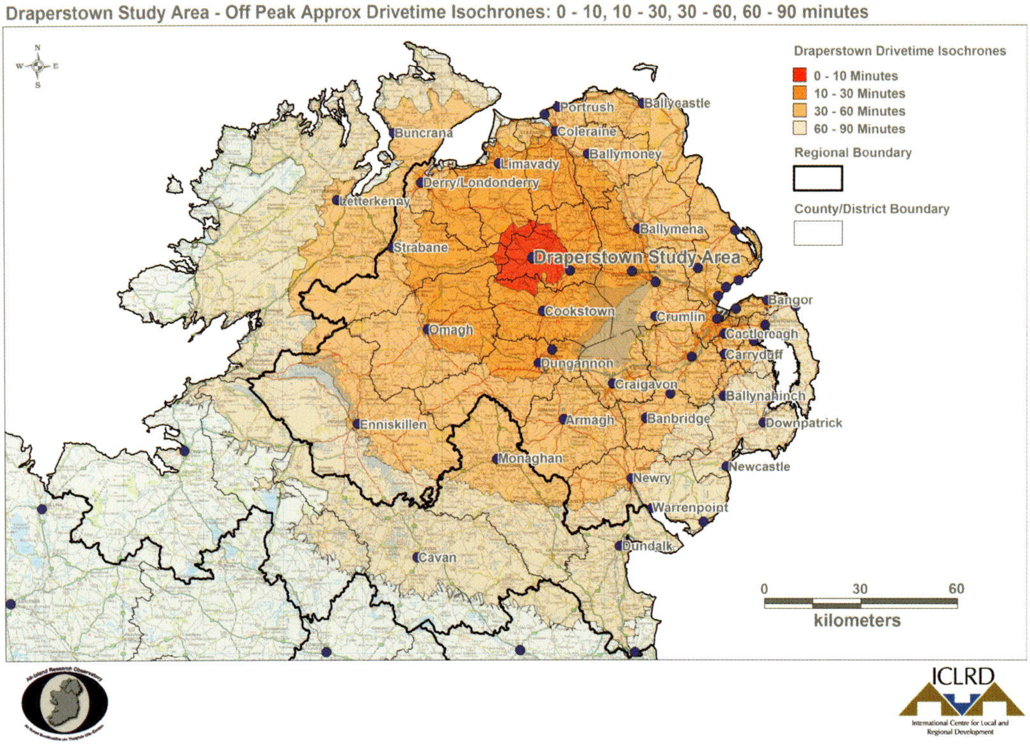

(Prepared by AIRO, 2009; © Ordnance Survey Ireland / Government of Ireland Copyright Permit No.MP000606)

Figure 3.2: Drivetime Isochrones for Emyvale-Truagh-Aughnacloy

Emyvale-Truagh-Aughnacloy Study Area - Off Peak Approx Drivetime Isochrones: 0 - 10, 10 - 30, 30 - 60, 60 - 90 minutes

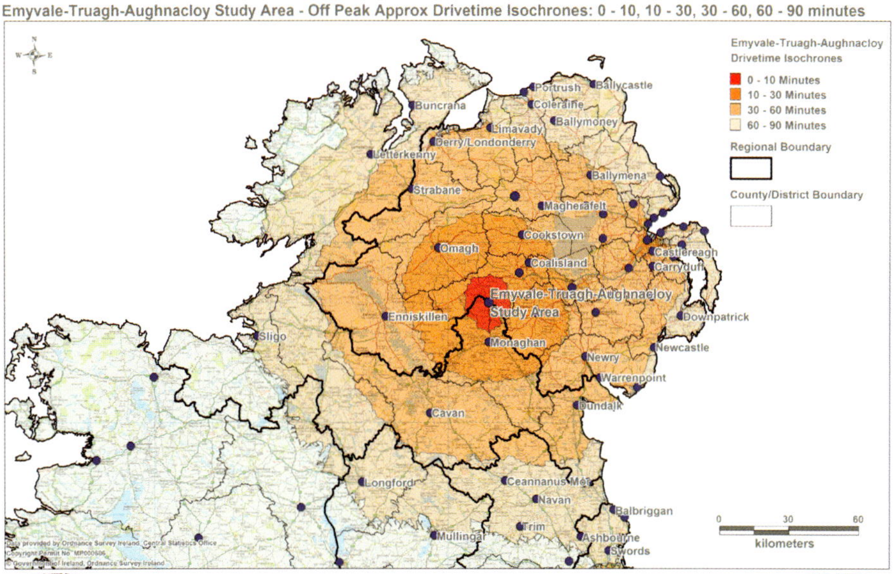

(Prepared by AIRO, 2009; © Ordnance Survey Ireland / Government of Ireland Copyright Permit No.MP000606)

Figure 3.3: Drivetime Isochrones for Duhallow

Duhallow Study Area - Off Peak Approx Drivetime Isochrones: 0 - 10, 10 - 30, 30 - 60, 60 - 90 minutes

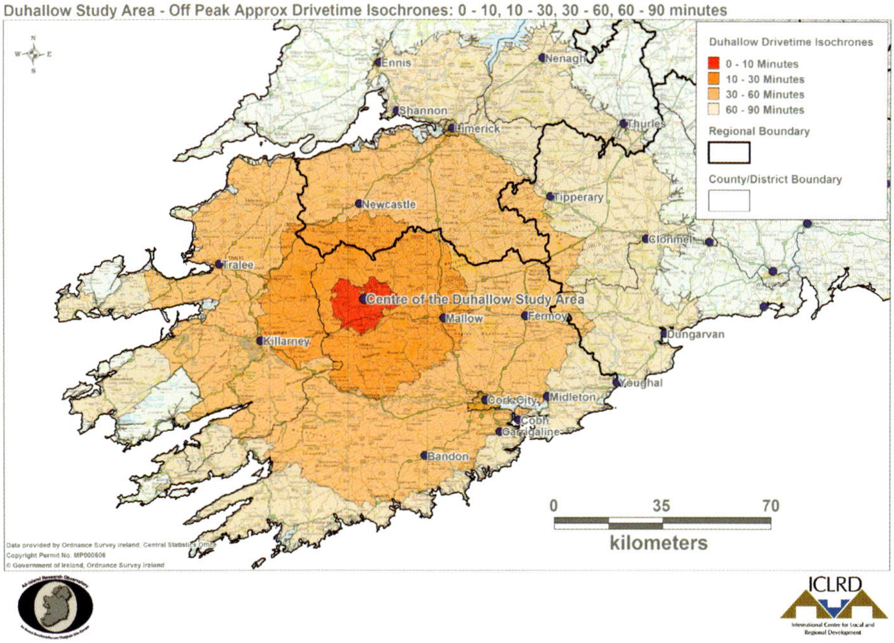

(Prepared by AIRO, 2009; © Ordnance Survey Ireland / Government of Ireland Copyright Permit No.MP000606)

PHASE 1 NOW ON RELEASE
Mullan Village
COUNTY MONAGHAN
www.mullanvillage.com
A breathtaking development of 1, 2, 3 and 4 bedroom homes with a superb turn key finish
Energy Efficient Homes
moneycare
'For The Best Mortgage Deals'
3 Dawson Street, Monaghan
047
PROPERTY PARTNERS
Gartlan
2 Dublin Street . Monaghan
047 72277
COONEY ARCHITECTS

CHAPTER 4:

Collaborative Governance and Sustainable Development

Key Messages

- Community engagement alone is not sufficient; rather there must be meaningful and committed participation from all stakeholders. This participation can come through a variety of means that utilise both formal and informal structures.

- Building into community groups the principles of, and the capacity for, good governance is an important aspect of community-based rural development companies. This process itself can be time consuming; but nevertheless, a progressive step-by-step approach is necessary as many community development organisations have previously failed because the organisational capacity did not exist.

"Local communities are the driving forces between the socio-economic development of their hinterlands – whether cross-border or not – and they do so with minimal financial backing. Such groups need to be given the recognition this deserves and applauded for the work they do; rather than criticised for standing on the toes of others".

(Research Interviewee, Emyvale-Truagh-Aughnacloy)

- Councils on both sides of the Irish Border have varying functions, are funded differently and comprise elected officials serving different terms of office; this results in it being extremely difficult to match like-with-like. An associated issue is the variances in data collection units and frequency, impacting on policy development and monitoring.

- Current performance monitoring systems within the public sector tend not to incentivise initiatives such as engagement in collaborative

governance or indeed inter-agency collaboration. These systems need to change so that public bodies are enabled to be more developmental rather than being deliverers of centrally-defined initiatives.

- **In terms of applying the micro-region concept, it is for each community and rural area to determine the scale and size of its micro-region based on the challenges faced and / or opportunities offered at a given time. The micro-region is better placed to respond to the opportunities that can be derived from urban-based development and secure the long-term viability of rural areas through complementarity.**

The successful delivery of rural restructuring, through revised socio-economic development trajectories, is deeply dependent upon the involvement of a range of stakeholders including the community and local / central government as well as businesses. Indeed, engagement alone is not sufficient; rather there must be meaningful and committed participation from all stakeholders. This participation can come through a variety of means that utilise both formal and informal structures. Going forward, there continues to be a significant role for the state as well as citizens and other stakeholders (see Table 4.1).

Table 4.1: Position of Key Actors in the Governance Process

Actor	Former Role	Contemporary Role
State	• Provider of public goods	• Facilitator enabling communities to govern themselves
Citizens and stakeholders	• Grant of electoral mandate to politicians; otherwise inactive	• Direct participation of citizens and stakeholders in governing activities

(Adapted from Woods, 2005)

4.1 Collaborative governance

The term 'collaborative governance' can be interpreted in various ways depending on the intellectual and policy context to which it is applied. In moving towards an understanding of how to secure rural restructuring on the island of Ireland, collaborative governance is concerned with an approach that is open, participatory and integrative. Furthermore, it is an approach which considers the need for locally-based responses to the challenges of economic development that complements the former top-down policy delivery agenda adopted by central government. Rural governance across Europe has reached this point through five key changes, most of which are demonstrated on the island of Ireland:

1. Scaling back of state activities in rural government and the engagement of private and voluntary sector organisations in local government functions
2. Shifting of responsibilities from the state to 'active citizens' through partnership working on a local scale
3. Greater coordination of rural policy delivery, including the amalgamation of government departments and agencies and formation of partnerships between different tiers and sectors of government
4. Replacement of some specifically rural institutions in favour of regional bodies encompassing both rural and urban areas
5. Reforms to local government, including changes to the powers, finances and territories of local councils.

Previous policy interventions by central, regional and local government often led to alienation from the local communities which were in actual fact supposed to be beneficiaries; on other occasions the institutional and organisational capacity barely existed to support the form of development advocated by the contemporary policy agenda. Another hallmark of rural restructuring on the island of Ireland over the past two decades has been the extent to which communities have 'learned' how to 'do' economic development. This has often required a steep learning curve and was without any guarantee of success. In Duhallow, for example, the much vaunted concept of 'self-help' and collective community action was initially alien to the majority of the area's population.

Building into community groups the principles of, and the capacity for, good governance is an important aspect of community-based rural development companies such as IRD Duhallow. This process itself can be time consuming, yet a progressive step-by-step approach is necessary as many community development organisations have previously failed because the organisational capacity did not exist. Indeed, before communities, and in particular disadvantaged communities or individuals, can become involved in 'acquiring the know-how of development', the local group needs to undertake awareness-raising and animation actions so as to engage citizens and ensure local ownership from the outset. Community development is not linear; rather, there exists a five-stage cyclical process based around an emphasis on integration and complementarity as demonstrated overleaf (see Figure 4.1).

Figure 4.1: Development Complementarity in Duhallow

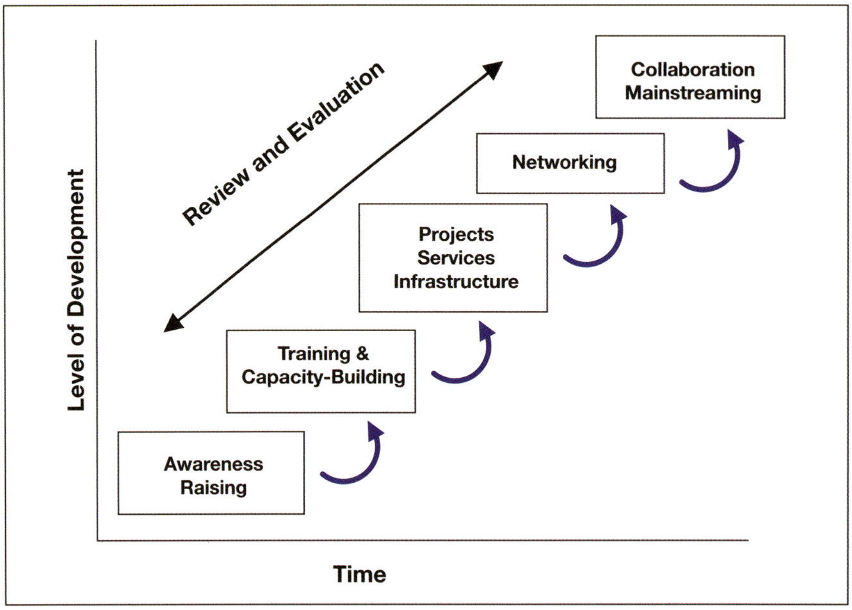

(Source: IRD Duhallow, 2004)

It is not only the micro-level community groups that need to operate under collaborative governance arrangements; this must also exist at the next level of development organisation as demonstrated through IRD Duhallow. The structure of IRD Duhallow's Board and Sub-committees has evolved considerably over time. This evolution has contributed to enhancing decision-making processes within the organisation, and has enabled greater numbers of citizens to influence and participate in local development and decision-making. There are significant benefits to be derived from such an approach including access to an increased level and range of resources, particularly funding opportunities that would otherwise not have been available.

Therefore, collaborative governance within rural development necessitates an integrated approach to organisational structuring. In practice this involves:

- Multi-annual business planning to guide implementation plans
- Sustainable approach to organisational structuring comprising thematic areas of development
- Democratic representation of interest groups on decision-making committees
- Overarching commitment to the development of social capital.

This approach to collaborative governance is successful because of an emphasis on process (organisation structure) as well as product or deliverables. This dual approach thus ensures community support and tangible outcomes; as operationalised by

Workspace in Draperstown (see Figure 4.2). Indeed, an emphasis on substance or output is crucial in the coalescing of participants, commonly around a number of key development factors including:

- A shared vision on how the area should develop
- Awareness of its 'potentiality'
- A 'champion' who is willing to bring the community together and push hard for action
- Being entrepreneurial and willing to take risks (not being hampered by lack of resources or finance)
- Recognising the value of education
- Ensuring there is an economic element to the plan for the area (that emphasis is not purely on social development).

At the same time, however, it is important that complex and unwieldy structures do not get in the way of action and delivery by the organisation. It is recognised that community-based economic development companies, such as IRD Duhallow and Workspace, are not ubiquitous in rural areas. In such circumstances where strong local development organisations do not exist, networks such as the East Border Region (EBR), Irish Central Border Area Network (ICBAN) and the Blackwater Regional Partnership play an increasingly important role in supporting and facilitating local governance and community participation. In the case of local government, for example, networks such as EBR and ICBAN provide opportunities for County Managers and Chief Executives of the respective councils to meet and discuss priority issues strategically for the Border region. Elected representatives also have the opportunity to come together and discuss identified needs, challenges and opportunities.

Moving further along the organisational hierarchy, structures must also exist for meaningful engagement with local and central government and allied agencies. As indicated above, these organisations can be enablers and facilitators for rural development. An issue arising here, however, is that rural areas are often peripheral to the catchment territories of state bodies, and in the current economic climate agencies are more likely to focus on large population centres than on rural areas. One response to this is the creation of a state-agency forum that brings together statutory agencies and the local development interests[9]. This offers a networking platform to share views, articulate local needs and can be a spring-board for collaborative working on both 'hard' (for example roads) and 'soft' (community) infrastructure. However, the significant challenge here is that current performance monitoring systems within the public sector tend not to incentivise initiatives such as engagement in collaborative governance or indeed inter-agency collaboration. These systems need to change so that public bodies are enabled to be more developmental rather than being deliverers of centrally-defined initiatives.

9. An example of this in practice is the forum established by IRD Duhallow.

Figure 4.2: Workspace Governance Model

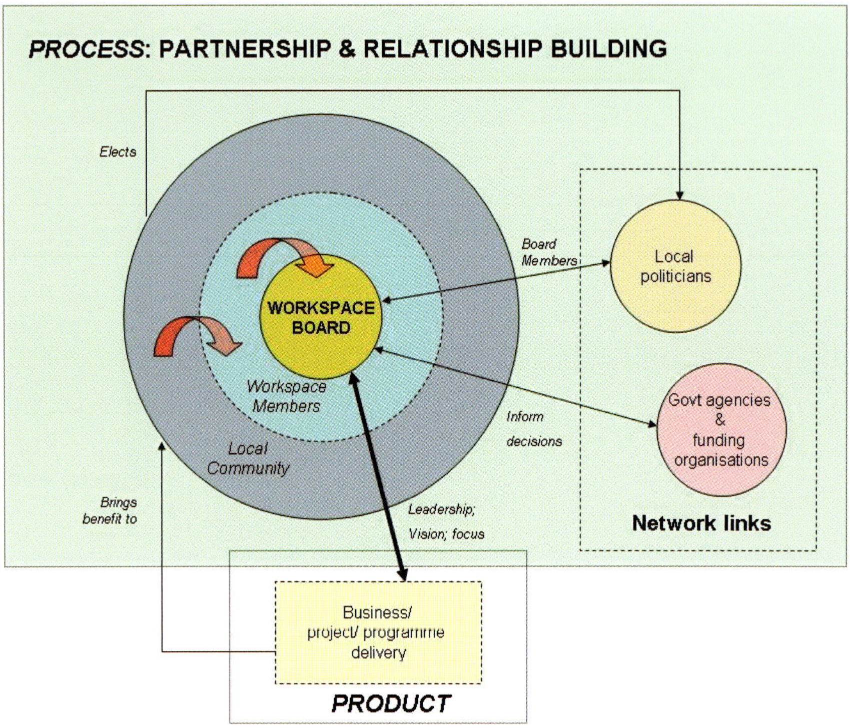

4.1.1 Barriers to Collaborative Governance

The local administrative systems, North and South, are at variance. Councils on both sides of the Border have varying functions, are funded differently and comprise elected officials serving different terms of office. This results in it being extremely difficult to match like-with-like; that is, matching council departments with the same or similar remit and matching personnel with the same or similar job description (Creamer *et al*, 2008). An associated issue is the variances in data collection units and frequency, impacting on policy development and monitoring. This discrepancy between functions is one of the main reasons put forward during this research for the comparatively low level of cross-border cooperation than could have been the case with greater complementarity between local government structures.

Councillors have been consistent supporters and advocates for the development of the rural...

Peripherality is also a barrier, as this can lead to disengagement from central government actors resulting in a fracture of the institutional arrangements necessary for collaborative governance. This further emphasises the difficulties encountered in the Irish Border region as described above.

4.2 Approaches to Rural Policy Making

Building on the messages emerging from **Chapters 2 and 3** of this report, there is a disconnection between state agencies and stakeholders / citizens; the reolution of which requires trust, relationship building and demonstrable outcomes for the local areas. Throughout the island of Ireland, the centralisation of policy decision-making and the lack of functional competencies at local government level (which vary between the two jurisdictions) raise concerns around the future population growth and sustainable development of rural communities. This raises two key questions:

- Who at regional and / or national level has a ***vision*** for the rural?
- Who at a regional and / or national level is effectively ***championing*** the rural?

Recognising the importance of the concept of 'rural champion', the Department of Agriculture and Rural Development (DARD) in Northern Ireland is in the process of developing this concept as part of their current rural development strategy (see **Chapter 2**). However, there is one grouping which it could be argued has a vision for, and has long been a champion of, the rural – and they are locally elected representatives, both North and South. Councillors have been consistent supporters and advocates for the development of the rural; ranging from service maintenance and provision to infrastructure upkeep (paving, roads, street lighting) to volunteering on local committees. However, while their intentions are good, the outcome of their actions and interventions do not always meet or 'fit' with strategic development objectives. This variance can be attributed to capacity issues and the need, going forward, for more and continuous professional education of councillors.

Visioning is a vitally important exercise across all spatial scales, one which has the potential to link across the hierarchy of plans that impact upon rural restructuring and development. Regional and national policy must conceive how the vision at a strategic level connects locally (top-down), and also vice-versa (bottom-up). At the same time, local communities must be enabled to have ownership of the regional / national vision and, of equal importance, commit to their role in the delivery of this vision through a partnership approach. Achieving a common vision across the spatial scales will require a communicative approach to policy development and innovative consultation mechanisms to meaningfully engage with the range of stakeholders.

Achieving a common vision across the spatial scales will require a communicative approach to policy development and innovative consultation mechanisms to meaningfully engage with the range of stakeholders.

4.3 The Micro-Region Concept

The concept of the 'micro-region' is not new, it is a term and an approach to micro-level development that is used in many countries throughout the world, including Mexico, Hungary, Czechoslavakia and France.

Central to the micro-region concept is a shift in community mindset and policy delivery from an area-based to inter-locality model. Adopting this model recognises that micro-regions are part of, and contribute to, their wider region. This change in conceptualising development in rural areas is dependent upon the suitability and quality of governance arrangements because of the integrated approach to planning that is necessary. In other words, this is a distinctive step-change to the silo-based policy approach that has to date hindered meaningful rural development across the island of Ireland. It is also a challenge to community organisations that hitherto have focused solely on growth within the boundaries of their own locality. The complex spatial planning policy environment that currently exists may not itself be radically altered – national, regional and local strategies will remain. Rather, the micro-region concept demands a (re-)connecting of stakeholders supported by the institutions of the state at national and local level, and a widening / dissipation of vision boundaries by community organisations (see Figure 4.3).

Much of what the micro-region concept entails is in actual fact coincidental with good governance approaches, such as:

- Bottom-up approach to local economic development that can form part of the wider region's growth
- 'Fit' with national, top-down structures
- Identification of the importance of local capacity as well as the identity and territorial integrity of places and communities.

Figure 4.3 Visioning in Rural Restructuring

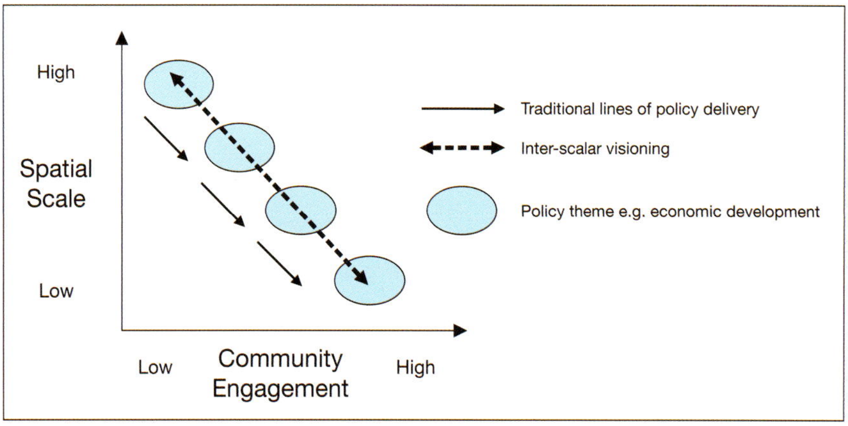

Internationally, the micro-region is considered to represent a space that is larger than the municipality and which can include districts, larger metropolitan areas and mega-cities (Baumgartner, 2008). However, for the purpose of this study – and given the scale of the island of Ireland – the definition of the micro-region is deliberately more fluid and dynamic.

It is for each community and rural area to determine the scale and size of its micro-region based on the challenges faced and / or opportunities offered at a given time. From the geographical perspective, a micro-region is an area that is an aggregated group of townlands or Electoral Divisions / Wards; its scale is below the County / District level; and it can operate in a transboundary manner, be that traversing a county, district or international border. Good operational examples of transboundary collaborations include IRD Duhallow, which crosses the Cork-Kerry border, and the recent extension of the Fermanagh Marble Arch Geopark into County Cavan. It is evident from the research carried out for this study that there is no need for additional 'formal' administrative boundaries to be introduced – enough exist already, many acting as barriers to partnership and collaborative governance.

The advantage of utilising the micro-region as a way through which rural diversification and development can be facilitated means that its fluidity can vary over time so that particular needs can be addressed when necessary. The micro-region should function without a 'hard' boundary; it is to its advantage to maintain soft boundaries that can adapt to changing events and needs, and scale up or down when appropriate. This approach of 'fuzzy' boundaries has been adopted in a number of spatial policy documents and is increasingly becoming a more effective method of applying and adapting policy responses. For example, the spatial strategy for Wales adopted a conceptual approach to mapping its objectives for development and growth, allowing for more dynamic relationships between regions and collaborative networks among towns and cities (Welsh Assembly Government, 2008).

The adoption of a fluid definition of the micro-region also allows for groups and individuals involved in an area's development to adapt and to be as dynamic as possible. This is particularly important given the fact that the success of the micro-region is dependent on the local capacity of actors and stakeholders, and on the importance of top-down support. In reality, this means that given the needs to be addressed at a particular time, a wide number of agencies, groups and individuals can contribute when appropriate; therefore utilising the skills and expertise that already exist. Local champions of rural areas, including the aforementioned elected representatives together with volunteers and community leaders, are vital to the successful development (which may, or may not, entail growth) of the rural micro-region.

UNITS
A1 - A13
A2

CHAPTER 5:

Rural Land and Landscape

Key Messages

> *"How do we integrate the many facets and intricacies of our rural into a comprehensive rural development policy? How can we preserve these areas without making them antiquated?".*
>
> **(Commissioner Fischler, CEC, 2003)**

- **Severe environmental degradation since the middle of the twentieth century has accentuated the need for policy and strategic interventions to protect biodiversity and landscapes. In response, new approaches to balanced development recognise the environment as a collective asset that is not only important to certain economic activities but is also a factor in the quality of life that an area offers – and this needs to be safeguarded.**

- **Area branding such as that employed in the case study areas of Duhallow and Emyvale-Truagh-Aughnacloy, based on aspects of the natural environment, both strengthens cultural identity and gives local firms competitive advantage in marketing their produce.**

- **Area partnerships, including LEADER, have played a key role in enhancing local democracy by involving community and voluntary groups in local decision-making. They not only promote bottom-up strategy development but also bottom-up delivery. Many projects supported by these local partnerships have emphasised the integration of natural resources into broader spatial and regional development frameworks - including rural tourism initiatives, village enhancement, heritage management and energy conservation.**

- **While Special Areas of Conservation (SACs), Natural Heritage Areas (NHAs), biosphere reserves and other designations represent a positive**

framework for the conservation of species, the preservation of our biodiversity relies on the health and extent of habitats in non-designated areas, and in particular in the wildlife corridors that connect Natura 2000 sites. In this respect, on-farm practices are of considerable significance.

- **The capacity of the countryside to absorb the current trend in single rural house building is becoming increasingly diminished given the vulnerability of the groundwater system throughout the island and the need for construction practices to move towards lower carbon / carbon neutral emissions.**

- **Under the promotion of agri-environmental initiatives, farm plans need to be integrated with environmental initiatives outside the farm gate. In addition, plans on adjoining holdings ought to complement one another and form part of the process of enabling micro-regions to attain the status of bio-regions, as occurs in the Alpine states and in parts of France, Germany, Spain and Northern Italy.**

Environmental conservation and sustainability are central to any successful balanced development strategy. Traditional, exogenous and industrial approaches to development tended to find it difficult to resolve conflict between economic development and ecological sustainability. However, neo-endogenous, localised approaches (such as the micro-regional) tend to place considerable value on natural resources and to incorporate the 'natural' into area-based development strategies and processes. Indeed, such approaches emphasise environmental competitiveness on a par with economic and socio-cultural competitiveness.

Severe environmental degradation since the middle of the twentieth century has accentuated the need for policy and strategic interventions to protect biodiversity and landscapes. While public authorities retain an important function in defining the parameters of human activity in respect of resource exploitation and in implementing corresponding legal frameworks, new and complementary approaches to the valorisation of natural resources have emerged that involve a proactive role for local actors, and in particular for civil society. These new approaches consider the environment as a collective asset; which whilst being essential to certain economic activities, is also a factor in the quality of life that needs to be safeguarded for current and future generations. There is a growing acknowledgement that not all communities wish to plan for growth; rather they place emphasis on quality of life and using their existing resources to generate an income (for example, the richly varied landscape that is the Fermanagh Lakelands). As a result, natural and heritage resources have acquired unprecedented value due to the image they create and the way in which they contribute to the aesthetic quality of the living environment in terms of landscape, architecture, town, village and countryside planning and amenities.

5.1 Capitalising on an Area's Natural Resources

Today, the environment is a key factor and resource in the competitiveness of rural areas. Preserving the environment and landscape of a locale means safeguarding that area's identity, distinctiveness and characteristics. This trend is set to gather momentum in the context of the restructuring of the global economy and the consequent renewed focus on localisation and sustainability. Indeed, the European regions with the highest levels of economic competitiveness are no longer exclusively the core agglomerations such as the 'Pentagon'[10], but are also those regions – many rural – that associate regional and micro-regional identity with the rural environment, and base economic development strategies on the innovative utilisation of local resources; for example, food production and research in the Catalonia and Aragon regions of Spain.

The process of the increased valorisation of natural resources is marked by a partnership approach and a consultative style of management. These emphasise landowners' responsibilities to society and involve incentivising protective measures. Conflicts over conservation are reduced or eliminated by decentralising decision-making and by involving the maximum number and range of local stakeholders in the management and conservation of natural resources. Area branding for example, based on aspects of the natural environment, both strengthens cultural identity and gives local firms competitive advantage in marketing their produce. There are many examples of this throughout the island of Ireland; not only in the case study areas (see Box 5.1) but also in neighbouring territories such as the Green Box labelling system for ecotourism which is being applied to certain parts of the Irish Border region (see http://www.greenbox.ie/quality-standards.php) and the Fushia Brand Initiative that is also being used for tourism marketing in West Cork (see http://www.westcork.ie/west-cork-branding-initiative.htm).

Box 5.1 Area Branding in Duhallow

The **'Duhallow' name** is used by several sporting, cultural and community organisations. This affinity with Duhallow has consistently been strong among the community sector. IRD Duhallow is responsible for the establishment of Duhallow Community Food Services and DART (Duhallow Area Rural Transport). DART bus-shelters place the Duhallow brand in every community in the territory. At the approach to every village, one is met with a large green sign with the name of the village and an image with the words 'Duhallow Trail.'

Area Branding in Emyvale-Truagh-Aughnacloy

The **'Blackwater' name** is increasingly being used by this border community to brand and market itself on a cross-border basis. The Blackwater Regional Partnership has, over the past fifteen years, worked with the communities in the wider region to develop initiatives which will put this area 'on the map' and attract both visitors and investors to the region. Walking and rambling clubs in the area have grouped together to develop the 'Blackwater Rambling Programme'. Other local businesses in the area have used variations of local townland or parish names; in Truagh, for example, businesses include TruWood (furniture-making) and Tru-Beginnings (childcare).

10. The EU 'Pentagon' includes the cities of London, Paris, Munich, Milan and Hamburg. As a proportion of the EU27 and acceding member states, approximately 32% of citizens live and work in this agglomeration (see http://www.vrom.nl/pagina.html?id=36865).

5.2 Landscape and the Area Partnerships

Area partnerships, including LEADER, have played a key role in enhancing local democracy by involving community and voluntary groups in local decision-making. They have, for example, animated and financed the implementation of social and economic-development projects; which in many cases are based on, and give effect to, the conservation of natural resources and amenities. Many projects supported by these local partnerships have emphasised the integration of natural resources into broader spatial and regional development frameworks - including rural tourism initiatives, village enhancement, heritage management and energy conservation. This has been done through capacity-building, training and awareness-raising actions among citizens, particularly with young people and the unemployed. Moreover, the partnerships have empowered communities to take responsibility for their environment and have prevented fragile rural, urban and peri-urban areas suffering environmental degradation. In Duhallow, for example, LEADER has initiated a number of projects to protect the land and landscape from the negative impacts of land abandonment. Across the island, area partnerships have demonstrated that responsibility is more important than ownership. This has been particularly important in the restoration of old buildings for community, commercial, or tourism purposes; the development of angling; and the re-opening, usually for recreational purposes, of old railway lines, canals, mills and mines.

Through their role as brokers, area partnerships can play an increased role in promoting the conservation of the rural landscape. The aforementioned Cohesion Process (see **Chapter 3**) which, for example, has included LEADER being integrated with local development and social inclusion, gives rural areas a governance structure with the capacity to interface with the productive sector (including landowners), local communities and statutory bodies in promoting collaborative approaches to environmental valorisation and conservation. However, many Partnerships need to become more promotive and proactive in this respect, and take the initiative in leading and co-ordinating conservation, preservation and enhancement projects.

5.3 Conservation Designation

The Europe-wide network of conservation sites that is *Natura 2000* presents a very significant opportunity for rural areas. It represents the new approach to conservation that emphasises complementary environmental, social and economic gain in the long-term. At present, there are 560,445 square kilometres within the *Natura 2000* Framework (EU-25); of which 10,561 and 25,109 are in Ireland and the United Kingdom respectively – accounting for just 6.3% of the EU total. While Special Areas of Conservation (SACs), Natural Heritage Areas (NHAs), biosphere reserves and other designations represent a positive framework for the conservation of species, the preservation of our biodiversity relies on the health and extent of habitats

Across the island, area partnerships have demonstrated that responsibility is more important than ownership....

in non-designated areas, and in particular in the wildlife corridors that connect *Natura 2000* sites. In this respect, on-farm practices are of considerable significance.

Farmers and rural communities in these and in other selected areas can potentially benefit economically and socially from such designation; provided, however, that selection is not imposed but is promoted through partnership; and is combined with information-dissemination, training, local governance and supports for economic diversification.

5.4 EU Directives and Land Use

At an EU level, a number of directives have helped to protect and conserve areas of pan-European importance. As members of the Council of Europe, Ireland and the U.K. are signatories of the Bern Convention (1979) on Biological Diversity. These pan-European initiatives, together with several United Nations protocols and conventions, provide a framework for national and regional environmental policies; they address transboundary environmental concerns and offer bases for cross-border collaboration to promote conservation.

Despite a positive international and supranational context, the application of environmental legislation on both parts of the island of Ireland has been tardy at best. Ireland's failure to implement aspects of the *Bird's Directive* (1979) alone has cost the Irish State over several million Euro, while individuals and consortia who have damaged ecosystems have not been made to repair the damage done. Thus, the public in general, and rural communities in particular, are paying a very high price for the recklessness and speculation of a few.

5.4.1 Housing

Planning decisions about rural housing in Ireland, North and South, have been a source of contestation for a number of years, provoking much debate about the future of the rural population. How people live in the countryside and their location have all come under question and are a major challenge to rural planning. The capacity of the countryside to absorb the current trend in single rural house building is becoming increasingly diminished given the vulnerability of the groundwater system throughout the island. There is an increasing need for construction practices to move towards lower carbon / carbon neutral emissions. In addition, decisions regarding housing and all other types of development in the countryside will be more strongly driven by EU Directives, with the *Habitats Directive* (CEC, 1992), the *Water Framework Directive* (CEC, 2000) and the subsequent *Groundwater Directive* (CEC, 2006) set to become the predominant guidance on rural planning into the future. Generally, responses to climate change such as those required by the Kyoto Protocol calls on all nations to live more sustainably by lowering emissions from construction, agriculture, transportation and so on. Future development in urban and rural areas will be determined by these Directives and the hierarchy of plans discussed in previous chapters will be required to adhere to these. For rural housing in particular, where individual septic tanks are the dominant sewerage type, the new *Groundwater Directive* will require that pollution trends are reversed by 2015 and that measures are put in place to prevent or limit inputs of pollutants into groundwater.

5.4.2 Farming

As previously noted, agri-environmental schemes have operated across the EU since the McSharry Common Agricultural Policy (CAP) Reforms in 1992. How these schemes operate below the European level is decided and managed by each individual member state. In the Republic of Ireland, the Rural Environmental Protection Scheme (REPS) was introduced in 1994. In Northern Ireland, a number of agri-environmental schemes have operated in recent years, including the Countryside Management Scheme (NICMS) and the Environmentally Sensitive Areas Scheme (ESAS). Predicated on the EU's advocacy of multi-functional agriculture, each jurisdiction's schemes incentivise farmers to be both commodity producers and guardians of the countryside. Initially viewed with scepticism by some of those with a vested interest in productivist agriculture, REPS has generally proven to be a successful initiative in the South (Crowley *et al.*, 2008). Such initiatives have enabled farmers, particularly those with smaller holdings to increase farm viability, while promoting conservation, improving local citizens' quality of life and providing resources for local economic diversification.

However, the promotion of agri-environmental initiatives has tended to be top-down and fragmented. National authorities on both sides of the Irish Border need to strengthen and mainstream their respective schemes, particularly as farmers face becoming subject to world prices post-2013. Moreover, farm plans need to be integrated with environmental initiatives outside the farm gate, while plans on adjoining holdings ought to complement one another and form part of the process of enabling micro-regions to attain the status of bio-regions; as occurs in the Alpine states and in parts of France, Germany, Spain and Northern Italy. Thus, the promotion of schemes such as REPS and NICMS must be inter-agency (not just reliant on Teagasc in the South or the Agri-Food and Biosciences Institute (AFBI) in the North) and criteria must adapt to local features, resources and economic development potential. There is a clear need to reduce agriculture's dependence on fossil fuels, feed and fertilizer imports, chemicals and the supermarket multiples by fostering the local food economy and by shifting the bulk of financial resources from Pillar I to Pillar II of the CAP. Indeed, collaboration at the EU level between DG Agri and DG Regio of the European Commission, and between the relevant national ministries / departments, is necessary in order to re-align policy objectives so that inter- and intra-territorial equity of opportunity is promoted in a sustainable manner.

...decisions regarding housing and all other types of development in the countryside will be more strongly driven by EU Directives

5.5 Rural Landscape Heritage

Many towns and villages throughout the island of Ireland have distinctive cores or structures that are worthy of protection. Such structures are, for the most part, noted in the County / District development plans and awarded protected status; the legal status of which has been greatly strengthened in Ireland by Section 81 of the *Planning and Development Act 2000* and in Northern Ireland by the *Planning (Northern Ireland) Order 1991* and *Planning Policy Statement (PPS) 6: Planning, Archaeology and the Built Heritage* (Department of Environment, 1999). Under these legislative frameworks, architectural conservation areas can be established as part of the development / area plan process; their objective being to preserve the character of a place, area, group of structures or townscape for their architectural, historical, artistic or cultural interest and value.

At a more local / community level, a further mechanism worth noting which not only helps reverse the widespread erosion of distinctiveness, but also is a means of involving local communities more fully in assessing the character of their localities and determining the type of design that would be appropriate for new development, are Village Design Statements (VDSs). Used properly, and where relevant tied in with architectural conservation areas (ACAs) that apply to village cores or townscapes, VDSs are an effective way of protecting, celebrating and enhancing local distinctiveness. Supports are available to assist communities in the preparation and roll-out of such programmes; namely through local councils and the Heritage Council of Ireland.

5.6 Land-Use and Rural Restructuring

Landscape and heritage are dynamic; they have been transformed and are transformable. Human interaction with the natural environment can be positive whereby local stakeholders make the most of their environment by making it a distinctive element of their area (AEIDL, 1999). This presents a dual challenge: conservation and revitalisation through creative management. New approaches to these challenges that emphasise decentralisation, collaborative governance, citizen participation, local responsibility and micro-regional development offer the most reliable route towards a win-win result.

McAULEY'S BAR

CHAPTER 6:

Economic Diversification and the Micro-Enterprise

Key Messages

> *"… SMEs are the lifeblood of our local and regional economies and we need to do what we can to ensure that they survive and create jobs and growth"*
>
> **(Cllr. Constance Hanniffy, CoR, 2009:10)**

- **Sustainable balanced development – including economic growth – is dependent on the contribution that small and medium size enterprises (SMEs) make to local and regional competitiveness and integration.**
- **It is local solutions – largely the result of indigenous entrepreneurship and innovation – which are key to the continued and sustained development (which may or may not involve growth) of rural settlements and the promotion of rural-urban interaction.**
- **Supports for micro-enterprise start-up or development – whether financial, training, mentoring, and / or facilitation – must be based on identified regional and local potential.**
- **Potential exists to increase the network of Business Innovation Centres (BICs) to cover the whole of the island – and this can be done on a strategic, functional basis; thus linking areas with similar traits and opportunities (i.e. micro-regions).**
- **To ensure greater clarity on who local business people should contact if they have ideas on how their business or locale / region could develop requires a streamlining of existing supports whereby surplus agencies are culled or amalgamated.**
- **Connectivity and accessibility are key to the development and growth of any business and in the current economic climate there is a strong**

case to be made for continued investment in hard infrastructure that improves both physical and virtual connectivity – roads, airports, ports and telecommunications such as broadband.

- **Areas with a lack of critical mass – such as the rural – are characterised by resources being spread too thinly across the ground. Through clustering, the pooling of resources can increase innovation and stimulate higher growth through raised productivity and improved linkages.**

- **The 'customisation' of training and upskilling is also a key element of SME development in the current economic climate. The *aspatial* nature of the existing skills strategies impacts (and not always positively) on the nature, location and duration of training delivered at the local level.**

Sustainable balanced development – including economic growth – is dependent on the contribution that small and medium size enterprises (SMEs) make to local and regional competitiveness and integration; such enterprises range from the micro-enterprise employing up to 9 people to the medium-sized enterprise employing between 100-499 employees. Approximately 1.2million new enterprises are created every year within the EU27 – the majority being SMEs – but only half of these survive beyond their first five years of operation. Yet today, SMEs account for 99% of businesses within the European Union (CEC, 2008). While the factors influencing the location of these enterprises are varied, it is increasingly acknowledged that regional policy – and in turn, its interpretation at the local level – impact on the attractiveness of an area for investment.

In mid-2006, Comissioner Danuta Hubner, with responsibility for regional policy, noted the increasing evidence pointing to the ineffectiveness of central growth strategies and that going forward "to be effective, they [*growth strategies*] must be integrated with tailored local and regional strategies"[11]. Almost three years later, in referring to the current world-wide economic crisis, Angel Gurria, OECD Secretary-General noted that this global contraction "is testing the capacity of regions to contribute with local solutions"[12]. Yet, it is these local solutions – largely the result of indigenous entrepreneurship and innovation – which are key to the continued and sustained development (which may or may not involve growth) of rural settlements and the promotion of rural-urban interaction.

The adoption and implementation of local solutions – and their impacts on spatial development – on the island of Ireland are, however, negatively impacted upon by the presence of an international border. While a number of rural cross-border areas can, and do, function as regional gateways and / or as commercial, service and administrative centres, the reality is that many remain peripheral and underdeveloped. The cause – and effect – of this underdevelopment is manifold, but includes having no clearly defined attributes on which to build / market the area as yet; poor infrastructure, in particular transport and communications; low levels of urbanisation; loss of, and poor accessibility to, services; low

11. Keynote address at the conference, *Regions for Economic Change: Innovating through EU Regional Policy*, Brussels, 12-13 June 2006 and reported in the Conference Proceedings Regions for Economic Change (CEC, 2006c).
12. Closing remarks delivered at the Ministerial meeting of the territorial development policy committee on 31 March 2009 (OECD, 2009).

employment rates with limited range of employment sectors; and low educational attainment. In addition, with conflict having been a recurring feature of the Border's history, potential investors have been frightened away. As a result, the growth of the rural economies in the Irish Border region including the case study area of Emyvale-Truagh-Aughnacloy – and to a lesser extent in the other regions on the island – have been highly dependent on the development and growth of local indigenous enterprises and the entrepreneurial spirit of the local population.

6.1 Micro-Enterprises in Rural Restructuring

Through diversification – whether through the creation of multi-farm products (on-farm diversification) or away from agriculture into areas such as service provision, tourism and the green economy – and in developing the inter-connectivity between rural and urban areas, rural communities have the potential to become hubs of innovation while continuing to offer a high quality of life; for example Cluster Holz & Technik in Italy (see Box 6.1) and Workspace in Draperstown (see Box 6.2). This in turn redresses the spatial imbalances between rural settlements and the surrounding larger urban centres.

Box 6.1 Cluster Holz & Technik, Italy

In the alpine province of Bolzano, timber construction and wood products are a traditional part of the local economy. Companies, however, over the years found themselves unable to compete with globalisation processes and external competitiveness. The sector recognised that to survive it needed to modernise – not only in technological terms but also in terms of how it marketed its products.

In response, the regional authorities encouraged the local businesses to establish a cluster; through an open call, SMEs were invited to submit cooperation projects aimed at promoting innovation. Initially, eight projects were financed – involving 28 companies – focusing on areas such as acoustics and lighting, development and marketing of ergonomic furniture, and furnishing for the wellness industry. At the same time, a number of horizontal actions were rolled-out. These included participation of local companies at international trade fairs, organisation of study visits, training on new technologies, the development of a business database, and the organisation of regular workshops and events.

Today, the cluster involves joiners, architects, carpenters, designers and sound technicians. By the end of 2006, the cluster included 175 members – mainly small family-run enterprises with a low innovation profile. However, by coming together, the members cooperate on new innovations in their respective fields.

Of the eight originally funded initiatives, seven are continuing without funding – and further projects are planned

(Source: European Commission, 2007)

mainstream education. This should involve action learning (through existing schemes such as work placement or the transition year 'Step into Marketing' module) or the wider roll-out of the Schools Business Partnership Student Mentoring Programme that is currently being delivered in targeted schools in disadvantaged areas in the Republic of Ireland.

6.1.2 Necessary Infrastructure

Connectivity and accessibility is key to the development and growth of any business and, where feasible, the subsequent clustering of companies. In this context, the rural-urban relationship is of increasing significance. A good quality road infrastructure and access to a larger urban centre is representative of having access to a wider range of services and opportunities (Dijkstra & Poelman, 2008) – as well as market-base – and together, these aspects impact on an area's capacity to attract and retain people; and therefore businesses.

In the current economic climate, there is a strong case to be made for continued investment in hard infrastructure that improves both physical and virtual connectivity – roads, airports, ports and telecommunications such as broadband. The poor quality and provision of broadband services in rural communities throughout the island is of increasing concern to rural businesses as it hinders them in overcoming geographical distances and access to people and, as a result, is detrimental on their ability to do business (sales, marketing, innovation, design). And this in turn negatively impacts on their capacity to compete globally. While the whole of Northern Ireland is purported to have access to a good quality broadband service, there are concerns within rural communities that the strength and speed of the service is not sufficient to support local enterprise. In the Republic of Ireland, the ongoing programme by the Irish Government to address this infrastructural deficit, through the National Broadband Scheme, is broadly welcomed – but there are concerns that the speed and strength of the resulting service will also be insufficient to support rural business development.

6.1.3 Rural Entrepreneurship and Spatial Planning

Spatial planning accommodates and provides for rural development including its organisation and provision of economic activity (Callanan *et al*, 2004). Through the planning process – and the hierarchy of plans and associated visions and policy objectives – it is recognised that not all places are the same and, therefore, different policies are required to develop different communities – whether urban or rural. At the same time, it is equally recognised that there must be consistency between visions and policy at the local level and those at a regional and national level, including the *Regional Planning Guidelines* (RPGs), the *National Spatial Strategy* (NSS) and the *Regional Development Strategy* (RDS). In the recently published Irish *Planning and Development (Amendment) Bill 2009*, for example, it is noted that in the preparation, making and variation of a development plan, the County

> *... it is recognised that not all places are the same and, therefore, different policies are required to develop different communities ...*

Manager's report will have to indicate clearly the extent to which the draft plan complies with the NSS and RPGs. This integration of plans, that are formulated in the context of collaborative governance and are based on vision rather than trend planning (including those covering cross-border catchments) – and which in turn meet local needs – position rural communities to better contribute to regional and national growth.

The challenges for rural development policy – and therefore, spatial planning – are to unleash the potential of rural resources (which are not always recognised), improve the balance between economic and social development opportunities and safeguard the quality of the natural environment for future generations. In terms of existing local policies to this end, there is a variance between the approaches adopted in Northern Ireland and Ireland. For example, Draft *Planning Policy Statement 4: Industry, Business and Distribution* promotes the location of enterprises on zoned land in Northern Ireland's towns and villages rather than in the open countryside (Department of the Environment, 2003). PPS4 argues for the restriction of development in rural areas in the interest of rural amenity and that land should not be zoned for industrial or business development in the interests of flexibility in small rural settlements. This, of course, has implications for business start-ups in rural areas. In the South, policy for light industry is ahead of Northern Ireland in that it is less regulated and more flexible regarding the location of such development types. This has been attributed to the recognition at the county level that the rural economy has always been based on individuals, sometimes employing one or two 'locals'. Therefore, policy has to be more innovative and flexible so as to capitalise on this 'entrepreneuralism'; as demonstrated in the *County Monaghan Development Plan 2007-2013*.

©IRD Duhallow

In terms of spatial planning policy, there needs to be greater coherence between the hierarchy of plans – both vertically and horizontally as well as on an inter-jurisdictional basis – and increased opportunities for integrated planning at the scale of the micro-region (thus taking cognisance of natural hinterlands).

6.2 Business Networks

In the context of the current economic climate, there is a growing interest in the concept of business networking and clustering throughout the island of Ireland. During the course of its field research, the ICLRD found this to be particularly true of businesses located in the Border region. It is recognised – and understood – that clustering can be applied to a wide range of activities, ranging from the more traditional to the high-tech and that the innovativeness of the cluster does not only apply to the type of activity but also to the operational procedures of that company. But, as noted by Dr. Karin Markides, Deputy Director General of the Swedish Governmental Agency for Innovation Systems (VINNOVA), a key feature behind the success of business clustering is "the provision of sector-specific and long-term financial support in the form of seed capital"[13]; this will not only stimulate research and development but promote innovation and creativity within micro-enterprises. It is further understood that both networking and clustering will not happen overnight; that it requires a long-term strategy involving both the private and public sectors – and ideally, regionally based universities or research institutes.

13. Input to workshop – Nurturing Local and Regional Clusters: The Role of the Public Authorities – as part of the conference *Regions for Economic Change: Innovating through EU Regional Policy*, Brussels, 12-13 June 2006 and reported in the Conference Proceedings Regions for Economic Change (CEC, 2006c).

Areas with a lack of critical mass – such as the rural – are characterised by resources being spread too thinly across the ground; resulting in its end impact being sub-optimal and there being little strategic focus (BMW, 2005). Through clustering, the pooling of resources can stimulate higher growth through raised productivity and improved linkages. The capacity for innovation within the specific sector is also increased – not only in terms of product development but also in terms of organisational structure and process. Scope exists to develop business clusters in a wide range of sectors; ranging from service provision (such as health, tourism), ICT, international services, biotechnology and biopharma (BMW, 2005; Department of the Environment, 2003).

A key role of business networks is to facilitate the exchange of information to the benefit of all members of the grouping. Collaboration leading to the generation of local innovation, the creation of partnerships and the development of the capacity of members is a central process within any network.

Third-level education institutes – whether universities, Colleges of Further Education or Institutes of Technology – play a key role in the development and success of business clusters and networks. In the global market, Research and Development (R&D) is increasingly important – as is the provision of research facilities and incubation spaces in an innovative and creative environment. Universities across the island of Ireland are increasingly providing such spaces, for example University of Ulster's UU Tech; as are the Institutes of Technology – for example CREDIT, the Centre for Renewable Energy at Dundalk Institute of Technology, and EpiCentre, the Electronics Production and Innovation Centre at Letterkenny Institute of Technology. The expansion of third-level outreach and access programmes are important in enabling rural dwellers and rural businesses to upskill and retain economic competitiveness.

6.3 Knowledge Economies

Given that innovation is borne out of the sharing of knowledge, one should not be astounded by the fact that the local knowledge base of an area has the potential to contribute greatly to effective development policy and practice; through revealing comparative advantage and how it can best be exploited (see **Chapter 3**), and emphasising the resources and assets present in the locale.

It is well documented that innovation activity tends to be highly concentrated, usually in large urban centres. Unless greater emphasis and attention is given to the rural-urban inter-relationship, as discussed in **Chapter 3**, there is a risk that such concentration could lead to further socio-economic disparities between urban and rural areas. To avoid this, the good practice that exists around knowledge transfer, innovation, networking and clustering needs to be disseminated while, at the same time, acknowledging that not all knowledge economies will be in a position to locate in the rural; urban-based jobs will, therefore, play an important role in sustaining rural economies.

The 'customisation' of training and upskilling is also a key element of SME development in the current economic climate. The *aspatial* nature of skills strategies – for the most part produced at a national level – impacts (and not always positively) on the nature, location and duration of training delivered at the local level. With the loss of jobs across all sectors but particularly in the construction industry and associated trades – joinery, electrical, plumbing – there is an increasing onus on national government to increase the number of training places available and revise legibility criteria. In addition, providers must adapt the courses on offer to meet local needs and local job opportunities (both potential and real) and provide training in accessible venues and at times that suit the clients.

6.4 The Green Economy

In the past year, there has been a growing global interest in the 'Green Economy' and the role that this sector could play in addressing the economic and environmental challenges facing the world at large. In the context of the island of Ireland, there can be no doubting that both jurisdictions are uniquely placed, in terms of its abundant renewable energy sources, to tap into this growing global market. In late May 2009, the Irish government set up a task force to focus on the development of Ireland's 'Green Economy' while in Northern Ireland, the Department of Employment and Learning (DEL) is paying particular attention to the skills requirements for this growing sector. With the potential to play an important role in the development of rural economies, nurturing the green economy should not, however, be regarded as a role primarily for the agricultural sector (through growing of biofuels for example). Rather, the opportunities arising from the green economy span a number of existing sectors; ranging from construction (carbon neutral housing and commercial developments) to the harnessing of wind and wave energies to sustainable waste management to ecologically friendly transport systems.

6.5 Enterprise Animation

The fostering of new enterprise development and the promotion and facilitation of enterprise networks are human resource intensive and, as such, require the guidance and inputs of development officers – in much the same way as the process of community development. An animateur's (development officer's) ability to enable and empower potential entrepreneurs and to promote inter-business linkages is as important as any particular business acumen.

Unlike as was the case in the past, the development officer must ensure that there is skills transference to the local community – so in the event that they leave their post, the skills-set needed to keep the partnership or initiative going are not lost to the community. Moreover, in the case of a business network or chamber of commerce, the animateur should not be attached to any single business or set of businesses, but rather should endeavour to promote the collective needs and potential of all businesses in the area. This involves organising training, facilitating information-sharing, identifying opportunities for inter-business collaboration, promoting local branding and interfacing with service provides to enhance local infrastructure. Emerging and expanding businesses require access to capital; and grant aid is important in priming ideas and in enabling innovations to be translated into business activities and employment creation.

©IRD Duhallow

CHAPTER 7:

Sustainable Communities and Social Infrastructure

Key Messages

- The strength of the rural is its sense of place and identity; but this is also its weakness. It is this fear of losing their identity that can negate against a rural community collaborating or networking.

- Vibrant community groups that are open, transparent, networked and linked to local governance structures are a vital component of rural community infrastructure, and experience to date points to the need to increase investment in community development.

- The 'rural' cannot be considered in isolation from the 'urban'; rather the complementarities and dependencies between each should – and will – inform the (permeable) boundaries of functional areas.

"A weak project or initiative can succeed in terms of tangible, positive outputs if there is a strong working group in support to drive it forward; a strong project or initiative – no matter how good in concept – will, however, fail if the working group is weak."

(Research interviewee, Draperstown)

- The economic downturn and rise in unemployment opens up new opportunities for volunteerism; a 'new thinking' needs to be developed in the context of how the unemployed can be used to support rural / community development.

- The scale of the micro-region is essential to enabling participative governance to function and the respective internal development associations to recruit able leaders; target, support and animate vulnerable persons and groups; and work to advance peace-building and cross-community relations. The micro-region has the potential to promote

volunteerism in a way that county or regional-based organisations do not have the flexibility to do.

- **The attainment of sustainable communities in Northern Ireland needs to involve peace-building, the elimination of sectarianism and racism and enabling people of different traditions to live, work and play together without fear or intimidation.**
- **Learning that is life-long and life-wide is essential in enabling rural areas to develop their potential economically and socially. Greater flexibility is needed in the way in which learning is promoted and delivered. There is a clear need to move beyond the traditional, institutional-based approach to learning, and to further resource and develop community- and firm-based approaches that offer flexibility in terms of delivery.**
- **Community-based services, social economy enterprises and outreach training and upskilling are essential in enabling rural areas to be more inclusive and socially progressive.**
- **Community / voluntary bodies must be 'plugged-in' to governance and decision-making structures going forward.**

The processes and forces of globalisation and rural restructuring have had profound effects on the social fabric of rural areas. The dissolution of boundaries and increasing access to ICT have opened up rural areas to new ideas and have brought about opportunities for social progress, networking and inter-territorial collaboration. At the same time, public service centralisation and the tendency by certain public bodies to focus services on centres of population is compounding social exclusion in many rural areas. However, a number of partnership initiatives involving local community groups and statutory service providers are tackling social exclusion and are succeeding in many instances in promoting a preventive approach to disadvantage; and the work of such agencies will become increasingly significant in the current economic downturn.

Rural areas, depending on their proximity to, and relationship with, urban centres will either take on (a) the characteristics of the peri-urban and be challenged to deal with infrastructural pressures; or (b) become more susceptible to out-migration, an ageing of the population, service depletion and growing levels of poverty and social exclusion. In addition to experiencing material poverty, people in rural areas can come up against barriers that preclude them from taking a full part in economic and social activities and exclude them from the decision-making processes. While the experience of rural communities has shown that a rising tide will not automatically lift all boats, the provision of social, physical and economic infrastructure can and does contribute to community development and the progression of individuals.

7.1 Social Infrastructure

Social exclusion in rural areas is associated with poor public service provision and a lack of commitment to rural-proofing in the application of public policy. In the case of public service and infrastructure provision, these are deemed essential in tackling rural depopulation, and by extension, isolation, loneliness and the rising suicide rate that has afflicted rural communities across the island. Transport and communications infrastructure, for example, enables economic development and diversification, and thereby provides opportunities for employment, training, personal development and outreach to vulnerable groups in society. Vibrant community groups that are open, transparent, networked and linked to local governance structures are a vital component of rural community infrastructure, and experience to date points to the need to increase investment in community development.

7.1.1 Community Services: Addressing Isolation

The economic liberalisation, which has characterised economic policy in both Ireland and the U.K. over recent decades, has achieved greater efficiencies in production, increased levels of participation in the workforce and considerable wealth generation, albeit disproportionately in spatial and social class terms. One of the features of the liberal economic model has been the general retreat of the state from the provision of community services in rural areas; although in parallel, the state has expanded its role as a regulator of service delivery. In respect of the former, the state's retreat from rural service provision since the 1980s, as characterised by the closure of rural post offices, amalgamation of schools and withdrawal of services from district / regional hospitals has left considerable gaps in many rural communities. Striking a balance between the financial necessity of these actions against wider social needs is complex. While these actions by the state have been economically unavoidable, the challenges to which they give rise must instead be regarded as opportunities; where communities can plug the resulting service gaps in a flexible and innovative manner. However, to bring these opportunities to bear, the state must play a role in facilitating and enabling local communities to take on this service delivery role; by so doing, this will ensure that those most in need are assisted and that the services are optimised, so as to support other strands of local development.

Examples of community led initiatives include the Blackwater Learning Centre, located midway between Emyvale and Aughnacloy. This provides an example of a community-run, agency-supported facility that provides training, community development, information, education and childcare services in an integrated manner. In Duhallow, the Community Food Service provides 'meals on wheels' to elderly people and those with disabilities over an extensive rural area. This project delivers tangible health and social benefits to the housebound, while simultaneously providing employment opportunities for people with physical and mental disabilities. In both Emyvale-Truagh and Duhallow, a rural transport scheme is operated which increases the opportunities for those living in rural areas, particularly the elderly, to access a wide range of services on a regular basis and to maintain contact with friends.

Empowering and resourcing communities to deliver and / or partner with the state in delivering local services contributes to ameliorating the negative effects of rural decline and advancing the promotion of social inclusion.

7.2 Culture and Identity

The strength of the rural is its sense of place and identity; but this is also its weakness. It is this fear of losing their identity that can negate against a rural community collaborating or networking. The valorisation and cultivation of local resources requires buy-in on the basis of territorial identity and cohesion; a development area should be large enough to promote inter-community networking and the involvement of external actors and, at the same time, be small enough to have a cohesive internal identity and external recognition of that identity. The Duhallow area in East Kerry and North West Cork, and the Blackwater Partnership catchment area straddling the North Monaghan-South Tyrone border are indicative of strong micro-regional identities. With twenty years of experience, IRD Duhallow utilised the recognition afforded this area as a basis for territorial branding (see **Chapter 5**), cultural development and the promotion of inter-community networking. Both micro-regions transcend administrative boundaries – one inter-county, the other international – but both are equally valid as micro-regional units (as outlined in **Chapter 4**). Rural development involves spaces that tend not to neatly fall within geographical administrative boundaries locally or indeed regionally. Furthermore, evidence from the research focus groups indicates that the 'rural' cannot be considered in isolation from the 'urban' (see **Chapter 3**); rather the complementarities and dependencies between each will inform the (permeable) boundaries of functional areas. As a result, workable governance structures that ensure effective horizontal and vertical linkages are a necessity.

©IRD Duhallow

Cultural resources represent a largely untapped dimension in rural development (OECD, 2005b), yet cultural affinity with a particular area is a contributory factor in defining a micro-region. The competitive positioning of rural areas in the context of globalisation and in the political arena requires emphasising the distinctiveness of local culture and traditions. Fostering traditional modes of expression such as literature, music and dance generates activities in rural and cultural tourism and has the potential to establish outreach initiatives by third level educational institutes, as demonstrated by the Rural College, Draperstown. This has served to stimulate economic development while also generating a greater sense of pride and 'can-do' attitude among local people. Indeed, there is a relationship between the promotion of traditional, local culture and the emergence of a spirit of entrepreneurism and innovation; as firms capitalise on local identity and branding, and collaborate with one another in order to maximise efficiencies.

Sustainable communities are realised by the integrated promotion of economic, socio-cultural and environmental objectives.

As well as promoting local and regional culture, rural communities face challenges and opportunities in embracing the traditions and modes of expression of newcomers, particularly those of migrant workers and other foreign nationals who have decided to make the island of Ireland their new home. While considerable progress has been made on this front in each of the three case study areas, newcomers are under-represented on decision-making structures and their empowerment needs to be advanced through refining local governance. This includes broadening existing community structures. One basic – yet effective – tool in bridging links within communities is the organisation of family fun days involving local community associations, sporting agencies and businesses.

7.3 Community Engagement

Participation in inter-community networks tends, contrary to much popular opinion, to promote rather than stifle local / community / village / parish identity. Indeed, community leaders report that collaboration with other community organisations and initiatives assists in the nurturing of the local community spirit. Community volunteers become more aware of their own local resources and capacity and this in turn motivates volunteerism and participation in development initiatives (see Box 7.1). Community engagement does, however, tend to be strongest at the micro-local level and going forward, increasing emphasis must be placed on raising local interest in county and regional development matters.

Box 7.1 Nurturing Community Spirit: Emyvale-Truagh-Aughnacloy

The Truagh Development Association spent over a decade building and nurturing its own association and community spirit before thoughts turned to cross-border collaboration. This entailed building up a strong leadership base ('champions') and engaging in short-term projects which resulted in tangible benefits – outputs that members of the wider community could see.

It was only when this community group had met its own immediate needs that it could turn its attention to cross-border and cross-community engagement – and as such, be more strategic in its thinking and actions. Working on a cross-border and cross-community basis involves breaking down barriers, challenging the persistence of a 'mental border', acknowledging the wrongs of the past and building bridges.

While fostering good relations, the cross-border communities of Truagh and Aughnacloy have been engaging in cross-border funded programmes – starting with PEACE 1 in 1997 – to demonstrate what can be achieved through collaboration. Initiatives to date include:

- The Aughnacloy Truagh European Studies Schools Project in 1997
- Blackwater Valley Broadband Consortium in 2004
- Vital Signs Project in 2005
- Opening of the Blackwater Valley Community Learning, Cultural, ICT and Peace Centre in 2007.

Having taken its time and nurtured relationships, the micro-region that is Emyvale-Truagh-Aughnacloy, centred around the Blackwater Valley, is now ready to broaden its network, engage further with Emyvale and source further funding to develop this area – socially, economically, culturally and environmentally.

In the case of the preparation of county / area development plans, there tends to be little community engagement at the level of the residents or community association – unless a controversial zoning or development is proposed. In the interests of strategic spatial planning and horizontal and vertical integration of 'visioning', communities must be encouraged to engage in county and regional development policies; and one mechanism through which this could occur is the community networks and forums. In the Republic of Ireland, for example, the existing Community and Enterprise Departments within the local councils could become a vehicle for increasing local participation in the planning process; by raising awareness among the community networks and forums of regional guidelines and policies, plan preparation and reviews, and local planning proposals.

7.3.1 Volunteerism

Governments, policy-makers, civil and religious leaders and political and social observers have expressed almost universal concern over the apparent decline in volunteerism, voter participation in elections, neighbourliness and social interaction in communities. The Irish Government and Northern Ireland Executive have promoted initiatives to foster social capital and civic pride and participation. Indeed, it was on the recommendation of central government that the Irish Central Statistics Office (CSO) included a question on volunteerism in the 2006 Census of Population; the first such question in a census in the Republic. The results showed that the highest levels of participation in voluntary activity are in rural rather than peri-urban or urban areas. Thus, rural development advances participation in community activities, and by extension, it advances democracy.

Exogenous support frameworks such as those advocated and promoted by the Task Force on Active Citizenship (2007) and by a number of local authorities, particularly in connection with *Local Agenda 21* (United Nations, 1992), represent positive advancements in fostering volunteerism. The economic downturn and rise in unemployment opens up new opportunities for volunteerism; a 'new thinking' needs to be developed in the context of how the unemployed can be used to support rural/

community development. Experience from the three case study locations in this research project also suggests the importance of voluntary bodies being 'plugged-in' to decision-making structures (see Box 7.2).

Box 7.2 Bottom-up Governance: IRD Duhallow

IRD Duhallow's extensive bottom-up governance structure provides communities with direct and indirect representation on its board of directors. This allows for a two-way flow of information between the partnership and local communities.

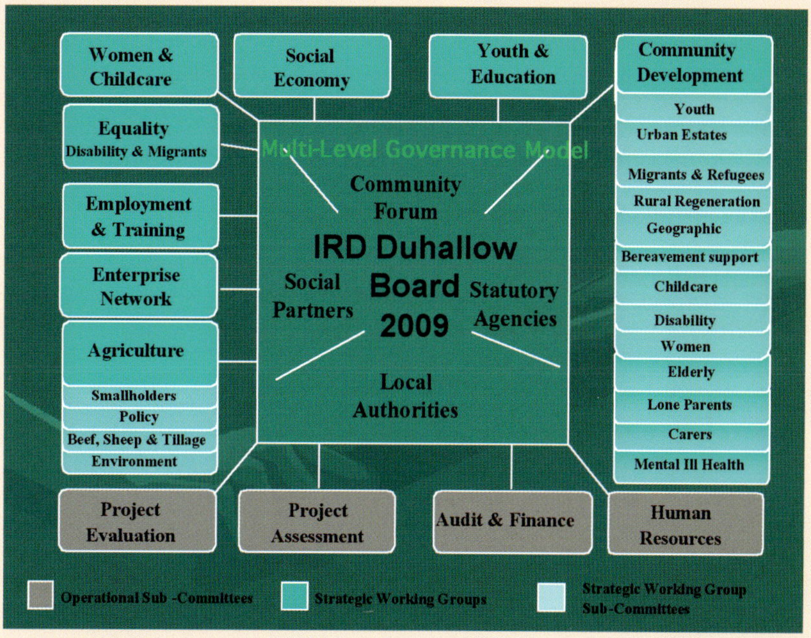

(Source Diagram: IRD Duhallow, 2008)

The scale of the micro-region is essential to enabling participative governance to function and the respective internal development associations to recruit able leaders, target, support and animate vulnerable persons and groups, and work to advance peace-building and cross-community relations. Their local base enables the micro-region to promote volunteerism in a way that county or regional-based organisations do not have the flexibility to do. Support for such endogenous initiatives, through on-going funding and through collaborative responses from the statutory sector, is essential.

7.4 Achieving Sustainable Communities

Sustainable communities are realised by the integrated promotion of economic, socio-cultural and environmental objectives. The successes of Workspace in Draperstown are largely attributable to its community business strategy, whereby the profits generated by economic activities are invested in facilities and services for the local community; for example, the leisure centre and after-schools club. As well as improving the local quality of life, this investment in social infrastructure provides spaces where people

can meet and socialise, and avail of training and self-advancement. In redressing the depopulation and rural decline that have affected their respective areas for several decades, both Workspace and IRD Duhallow have set about promoting new enterprise development and the expansion and networking of existing businesses. LEADER funding and the technical assistance provided by animateurs (see **Chapter 6**) and staff has been essential in this regard. In the case of IRD Duhallow, the Partnership's goal of improving demographic vitality has only been more fully attained since its enterprise strategy has been complemented by its social inclusion work and by providing community-based amenities such as childcare, eldercare and rural transport. New community groups (both geographical and communities of interest have also been established). In addition, existing community associations have been animated to recruit new members, undertake development projects and engage more effectively with statutory and local government bodies.

The attainment of sustainable communities in Northern Ireland needs to involve peace-building, the elimination of sectarianism and racism and enabling people of different traditions to live, work and play together without fear or intimidation. The EU-funded PEACE Programme, administered by Border Action, has enabled community groups in border areas to realise such goals; but there are notable concerns locally that the current re-orientation of funding streams away from community groups – towards larger entities such as local government – may not be as effective as locally-oriented and bottom-up initiatives.

7.4.1 Educational Capital and Skills Development

Learning that is life-long and life-wide is essential in enabling rural areas to develop their potential economically and socially. Education and training have been shown to increase regional GDP[14] and to ameliorate social exclusion (OECD, 2001). Greater flexibility is needed in the way in which learning is promoted and delivered. There is a clear need to move beyond the traditional, institutional-based approach to learning, and to further resource and develop community- and firm-based approaches that offer flexibility in terms of delivery. These can be tailored to local needs while attaining the highest standards. The current model of urban-based centres of learning is causing a brain-drain from many rural areas, resulting in out-migration of young people. Greater cognisance needs to be given therefore to the availability of outreach and life-long learning facilities in rural areas; for example, the Rural College in Draperstown and the aforementioned Blackwater Learning Centre in Truagh. With the potential to also encourage ongoing skills development in the local population, the issues of accessibility and connectivity to these rural centres, both virtually and in terms of public transport, must be addressed to increase the sustainability of these existing resources.

Various funding programmes, such as EQUAL, have enabled many rural areas to redress skills deficits. The level of success has varied depending on the resources available for animation and capacity-building, and the approaches taken by the relevant organisations. Thus, rural development actors, local authorities and statutory

14. GDP stands for Gross Domestic Product which is a measure of the amount of activity in, and thus the size of, an economy.

bodies need to be proactive and innovative, rather than passive and spatially-blind, when considering and planning for local skills needs. Going forward, agencies such as FAS in Ireland and the Department of Employment and Learning (DEL) in Northern Ireland need to work closely with the local area partnerships and local educational institutes in identifying local skills-needs of not only the businesses but also the unemployed and early school leavers, and determining the appropriate training programmes to be implemented in that area.

Learning that is life-long and life-wide is essential in enabling rural areas to develop their potential economically and socially

7.5 Social Inclusion and Rural Restructuring

Community development is integral to realising regional competitiveness and therefore, addressing local skills needs. Community and voluntary groups are emerging as significant players in promoting economic and social development, although current policy frameworks and practices among a number of state agencies fail to adequately acknowledge the contribution of community groups to local service provision. The top-down needs to be more constructive in responding to local level needs and decisions need to be joined-up. For example, the development of rural housing and the provision of training needs to be influenced by, and accompanied with, adequate public / community transport provision (both in terms of timing and frequency). Through the optimisation of locally-based public / community services, ecological footprints are minimised. In addition, by providing community-based services, social economy enterprises and outreach training and upskilling locally, rural areas are enabled to be more inclusive and socially progressive.

PART 3: Conclusions and Recommendations

ALL IRELAND CHAMPIONS
ARDSCOIL NAOMH COLM

CHAPTER 8:

Role and Potential of the Micro-Region

Key Messages

- Each rural area is unique and there is no 'one size fits all' model of rural (or urban) development.

- Key issues in the rural restructuring and regeneration process include the need for a strategic vision set within a top-down framework, delivered through partnership at local level, which embraces a holistic approach. This involves identifying and harnessing the local asset-base, supporting micro-enterprise development and networking, building local capacity and utilising the potential of the natural environment.

> *"Rural areas face several new opportunities and challenges which call for appropriate rural development policies and a more effective use of scarce financial resources".*
>
> **(Richard Hecklinger, OECD, 2006)**

- As communities change their perspective from focusing only on individual villages or townlands and conceive of the micro-*region*, it will be possible to change from a constant state of competition, both in business and for scarce resources, to cooperation that builds on critical mass, networks and economies of scale.

- A primary impact of the Review of Public Administration (RPA) in Northern Ireland – which will result in a reduction in the number of district councils and the further decentralisation of functions to local government – will be the increased compatibility between the workings of local government North and South of the Border.

- Going forward, both government (at its various scales) and community development policy needs to adapt to the changing economic climate;

and recognising that there are decreased resources available, greater emphasis needs to be placed on meeting local needs through harnessing local assets. This includes increasing supports for small to medium sized enterprises, providing for skills (re)training and putting in place appropriate social infrastructure.

- **To harness the potential of the rural, there are commitments and actions needed across a wide range of stakeholders; ranging from central government to the local development agency.**

Recognising that each rural area is unique and there is no 'one size fits all' model of development, this research considers the impact and future of rural restructuring policy and practice throughout the island of Ireland on people and place. Its key objectives include:

- Consider the potential role for asset-based / local endogenous development in rural restructuring
- Determine the role of rural restructuring in balanced spatial development
- Examine if the rural development visions as promoted to date have translated into on-the-ground action.

Economic diversification as a means for development is taking place in rural communities throughout the island of Ireland – some successfully, others less so. It is increasingly accepted that a range of mechanisms must be put in place to support those communities dependent on farming, manufacturing and construction but who, for various reasons, may wish or need to diversify. This includes providing advice on potential areas of diversification and establishing a flexible mentoring programme which is designed with *the specific needs of each particular area in mind.* Key issues in the rural restructuring and regeneration process include the need for a strategic vision set within a top-down framework, delivered through partnership at local level, and which embraces a holistic approach. This involves identifying and harnessing the local asset-base, supporting micro-enterprise development and networking, building local capacity and utilising the potential of the natural environment. Together, this will enhance people's quality of life and promote sustainable economic development.

Going forward, both government (at its various scales) and community development policy needs to adapt to the changing economic climate; recognising that there are decreased resources available, greater emphasis needs to be placed on meeting local needs through harnessing local assets. This includes increasing supports for small to medium sized enterprises (existing and new), providing for skills (re)training and putting in place appropriate social infrastructure. This report concludes that such structural changes should take place at the micro-region scale; a space of mutual identity within which resources are located, accessed, organised and utilised or conserved. For local development agencies and community associations, adopting a new operational model – such as the micro-region – is becoming increasingly essential as this is a model that has the potential to be flexible in responding to global economic change and the evolving needs of rural communities.

This chapter identifies the actions necessary – through recommendations – to enable effective restructuring in rural micro-regions and links this to spatial planning approaches on the island of Ireland.

8.1 Integrated Approaches to Asset-Based Development

A vision for an area has the potential to be a strong and effective tool in determining future growth and ensuring consistency among the various strategies emanating from the myriad of stakeholders involved in local development policy and practice. This potential, however, is dependent on there being continuity in the vision for an area across the various administrative and spatial scales – both horizontally and vertically. The vision must also allow for the participation of all key stakeholders in not only the rolling-out of the vision but also in determining its content at the very outset as part of an integrated approach to asset-based development.

8.1.1. Multi-Stakeholder Partnerships

Involving the community, particularly in visioning practices, is one component in the overarching governance environment that is necessary for sustainable rural development. Partnership is regarded as an element of an integrated approach to development. It is by necessity both horizontal and vertical, interfacing between the community and statutory sectors. This requires both visioning and commitment, often driven initially by a small number of key individuals, as demonstrated across all three case study areas; this being more complex in cross-border areas given the myriad of administrative boundaries. By broadening their community base, applying democratic principles and developing cross-sectoral linkages, bottom-up structures have – and can continue to - emerge as real drivers of local development.

The success of local partnerships is dependent not only on their being properly resourced but also on their having common interests and goals (based on a shared identity) and there being an effective communications strategy in place. This is key to ensuring local ownership. To ensure these various elements are in place, partnerships must be nurtured and trust developed; and this is not an overnight process. For this reason, partnerships must have short-, medium- and long-term objectives (see 8.1.4).

8.1.2 Capacity and Supports

The form of rural development advocated in each of the three case study areas is focused on deriving benefit not only for the local economy, but crucially also social advancement through community development. It is increasingly recognised that soft infrastructure has an important role to play in rural development. Success on many occasions is attributable to members of the community getting involved and bringing to projects and initiatives their energy, creativity and commitment. There is a need, then, to invest in social capital of a type where differences in religion, identity, and political viewpoint are not compromised but are complementary, serving to support and augment community cohesion rather than being a source of division.

In the current economic climate, where resources are limited, it will become increasingly important for local stakeholders to work together thus making best possible use of whatever resources are available. With various EU programmes changing and / or coming to an end and there no longer being the resources nationally to support multiples of similar projects throughout the island, increasing emphasis must be placed on the sustainability and mainstreaming of activities and partnerships. Such partnerships should not only consist of various community groupings but also of local government and business interests. The fracture that exists between community and government must be addressed – as each is now dependent on the other; not only for resources but also for the provision of services.

©IRD Duhallow

Even with institutional support and funding mechanisms, the *capacity* for communities to engage in the processes associated with the partnership approach must be nurtured. The assumption that deregulation and / or light-touch regulation is good for economic or social development has been swept aside by the recent financial crisis, and the case for greater public intervention and universal service provision is gaining increased currency. In fostering vibrant rural communities, rural service provision merits renewed public sector support, as well as the expansion of third sector approaches via local partnerships. Furthermore, volunteerism and an active civil society are highly regarded as valuable public goods, and territorial partnership approaches have proven to be successful in fostering social inclusion and community participation in economic development and decision-making.

8.1.3 Improved Connectivity

Common throughout the case study areas is the identification of infrastructure as key to the success of development and economic diversification. Poor connectivity, both in terms of transport and telecommunications, in rural and peripheral areas is an ongoing challenge that both rural residents (irrespective of age or dependency) and entrepreneurs must contend with. Quality physical infrastructure including roads, public transport services and broadband connections are a necessity to the success and growth of small and medium sized businesses. Despite the current strain on public finances, investment in such hard infrastructure must continue unabated. In addition, and for effective delivery, there must be support, collaboration and joint working between public, private and community sectors; and in the case of the Irish Border region, this needs to happen on a cross-jurisdictional basis.

8.1.4 Taking the Long-Term Perspective

Securing tangible outcomes, through target setting for the stakeholders involved in both economic and community development, are essential for the ongoing support of initiatives. The end-prize is the sustainability of the organisation and deriving greater benefit for the community served. It is recognised, however, that considerable time and effort will be required to reach this stage in the lifecycle of rural development programmes and organisations; but that the potential rewards more than justify such endeavours.

8.1.5 Recommended Policy & Practice Change

National Level

- The development and growth of rural communities is dependent on quality infrastructure that both increases and improves connectivity and accessibility. Despite the current economic downturn, there is a need for the relevant government departments and statutory agencies to continue with key elements of the capital investment programme as outlined in the *National Development Plan 2007-2013* for Ireland and the *Investment Strategy for Northern Ireland, 2008-2018.* Not only should these programmes meet current needs but they should also meet anticipated future needs.
- Increased emphasis must be placed on the establishment of the North/South Consultative Forum – as agreed under both the Belfast Agreement 1998 and the St. Andrews's Agreement 2006. Such a forum would create a space for central government and local communities (civil society) to come together to discuss the challenges and opportunities faced by the island in its development.
- Under the current Cohesion Process, there is a very strong case to be made for removing the current proviso that Board members can only serve a three year term. It is felt that this weakens the Board of the area partnerships; in that sustainable relationships cannot be formed or a good working knowledge built-up.

Regional Level

- There is a strong case to be made for the delivery of capacity building training at the regional level. With limited financial resources available, it is of increasing importance that training is delivered through the medium of an overarching body who can determine 'what' training is needed 'where', that the right people receive training and where possible, that similar organisations are brought together to avail of the same course – thus making maximum use of available resources and generating economies of scale.
- A regional communications strategy should be adopted whereby notices on ongoing and / or completed projects, upcoming events including training, organisations seeking partners, new policy developments and so on are disseminated to all development agents in the region on a regular basis.
- A space must be created at a regional level whereby local elected officials from neighbouring towns, micro-regions and counties (including on a cross-jurisdictional basis in the case of the Irish Border region) can come together to debate the challenges and opportunities of the moment.

Local Government

- There is a role for local government in working with community agencies in identifying potential shared resources and facilitating their allocation on an equitable basis.

Community Level

- Recognising that there is a decreasing pool of resources available from central and regional government to support area-based initiatives, area partnerships must enter into agreements with neighbouring organisations, by using for example the micro-

region model, on the sharing of facilitates such as meeting and training venues and local capacities / skills-bases such as secretarial support and trainers / advisors.
- To nurture the partnership and to operate with a view to becoming sustainable and non-funding programme dependent, partnerships must revise / develop their work programme to include short-, medium- and long-term objectives and targets.

8.2 Entrepreneurialism & Endogenous Industry

Many rural areas continue to have a narrow economic base and tend to depend on established activities such as agriculture and manufacturing. These traditional bases of the local employment sector have resulted in the skills pool of rural communities being largely 'skilled manual'. On the other hand, however, through decades of self-help in the form of volunteerism and entrepreneurial activity rural communities have built up an extensive organisational and managerial skills-set including project management and leadership; securing local stakeholder buy-in; and forming partnerships and engaging stakeholders.

8.2.1 Entrepreneurial Spirit

The case studies demonstrate that in order to achieve development there is a need to pro-actively promote economic diversification and encourage an entrepreneurial spirit within the community. This 'entrepreneurial spirit' within individuals and businesses is a key strength of many rural areas. To bring this forward, there is a strong case to be made for each rural community to carry out a skills audit; thus raising awareness among the communities themselves – together with the various support agencies – on the skills set available and the gaps that need to be addressed.

8.2.2 Endogenous Potential

There is an increasingly strong need, particularly in the current economic climate, for both local entrepreneurs and existing businesses to develop future products around local assets; these could range from the local skills-base, the natural landscape, the area's culture and heritage or its 'eco' potential (whether tourism, energy or the wider green economy). There is also scope to adapt working practices and become more innovative in this regard also; there are growing indications that small-scale companies want to work in collaboration by sharing ideas and building knowledge so that the business community as a whole benefit. This includes, for example, joint marketing initiatives undertaken with a range of local stakeholder organisations. The generation of critical mass and economies of scale through such collaborative processes is central to the growth and attractiveness of an area in enterprise terms, and particularly in the more rural parts of the island of Ireland.

8.2.3. Networking and Clustering

Based on existing and emerging business 'groupings' in rural areas, there is a strong case to be made for the promotion of business networks and, to a lesser extent, clusters (particularly where the emphasis is on process rather than product). This would allow rural communities to achieve some scale and improve access to clients. To date, such groupings have occurred in an ad-hoc manner; with the result that each business operated independently and limited networking took place. There is an increasingly strong case to be made for rural areas to consider how they can most effectively move away from their (over-)reliance on a small number of low added-value sectors. Such a move can broaden their economic base and generate more sustainable employment opportunities in areas such as the green economy and knowledge intensive industries.

For businesses thinking of engaging in a clustering process, the main challenge facing them will be the development of trust (they are after all moving from a position of being competitors to being collaborators). To develop this model, communities will need to bring in an external facilitator to work with them and identify common objectives and end goals that they wish to work towards. It will be important to take small steps at the outset; for example, through engaging in joint training around IT or health and safety. This will help build trust amongst the cluster. Other opportunities for collaboration exist around joint marketing and cost assessments (the objective of which is to reduce costs in running the business). Were a community to be successful in developing this business clustering model, it would undoubtedly be a model that the EU would be interested in showcasing.

8.2.4 Life-long Learning and Up-Skilling

There is a 'revaluing' of education taking place both locally and nationally. Greater emphasis is being placed on the achievement of third-level qualifications as well as in vocational training streams. Going forward, further focus needs to be placed on developing adult education and short training programmes which are based on an identified local need or issue; skills strategies can no longer be aspatial. The outreaching of training programmes to rural areas needs to be expedited; with initiatives relating to local potentiality and the stimulation of entrepreneurship.

8.2.5 Quality of Life

There is widespread agreement across both jurisdictions that the 'rural proofing' of government policies has, to date, proven ineffective. With the closure of services, there is little public evidence to suggest that the consequences of these actions have been considered (for example, if a rural school is closed, what distance do school-going children then have to travel to avail of the nearest school with capacity? and how is this journey to be made?). The objective of rural proofing needs to be reinvigorated – and there are indications that this is starting to happen. In addition, it is becoming increasingly clear in the current economic climate that the closure of unsustainable services – such as rural schools with declining numbers – is inevitable; and for those who make a lifestyle choice to live in the countryside, increasing consideration will have to be given to the fact that such a decision will increasingly mean having to travel to the nearby urban centres for certain services.

Job creation alone is not sufficient in redressing depopulation and in promoting sustainable communities. Over recent years, local development agencies have placed considerable emphasis on improving the quality of life in their respective territories; recognising that the territory needs to capitalise on the economic and social benefits that can derive from developments in nearby urban centres. To this end, communities are investing in the development and expansion of, or improving access to, childcare and after-schools clubs, as well as sports facilities and other recreational amenities. These elements of community infrastructure, together with the cultivation of social capital play a significant role in increasing quality of life and promoting rural regeneration.

8.2.6 Recommended Policy & Practice Change

National Level

- Future economic development policy on the island of Ireland should no longer place big emphasis on Foreign Direct Investment (FDI). Rather, the emphasis should be on indigenous enterprise, and in this regard, agencies such as IDA Ireland, Enterprise Ireland and Invest NI should be investing in, and developing strategies for growing, local indigenous enterprises.
- The functions of the myriad of enterprise support agencies needs to be clarified, and where there is significant overlap, organisations should be amalgamated or culled. The tradition within government of introducing new administrative layers – often in the name of simplifying procedures – without removing what existed beforehand needs to end as this is only leading to confusion on the ground.
- Broadband is key to the future growth and development of rural enterprises. The capacity and speed of the network throughout the island requires greater investment. The relevant government departments need to revisit their policies in this regard.
- The schools curriculum has a roll to play in nurturing entrepreneurialism and removing the 'fear' of becoming self-employed. While programmes do exist within, for example, Transition Year, there are opportunities to introduce business development programmes earlier – and across all schools (not only those located in disadvantaged areas). Such a curriculum should be developed in association with the statutory agencies such as Enterprise Ireland and Invest NI.

Regional Level

- The clustering of micro-enterprises needs to be nurtured and developed in association with the research and development centres in the third level institutes across the island of Ireland. This will not only enhance their innovativeness and creativity but ensure that they take a long-term perspective.
- There is a growing interest at the sub-regional level in the joint marketing and branding of local products. This should be overseen at a regional level by, for example, the regional authorities; agencies that have the capacity to recognise what areas / sectors should be collaborating and what opportunities, financial and other, exist to support such a strategy. Ideally, this action should take place in the context of their being a wider network of Business Innovation Centres (BICs).
- Further outreach facilities covering third-level and adult education, as well as up-skilling and (re)training, must be established to serve rural communities throughout the island of Ireland. Where possible, these should be located in appropriate

facilities in towns that serve a large rural hinterland, such as the Rural College in Draperstown, the Blackwater Learning Centre in Truagh, and similar facilities (where they exist) in the designated hubs or regionally significant centres. The establishment of outreach centres and the type of courses to be delivered in each should be determined by the appropriate third-level institute in association with the local authority and education / training agencies and representatives from the community network.

Local Government
- While clustering of small-scale enterprises is taking place throughout rural Ireland, few are engaging in network activities. This needs to be addressed and this is a key function for the economic development departments of local government.

Community Level
- Each community group should carry out a skills audit of itself and its wider community; this will identify the strengths and weaknesses of the agency and community at large in terms of capacity and clarify in what areas training are required. As well as addressing the aspatial aspect of national skills strategies, this will also assist the relevant support agencies in determining what training needs to be targeted to specific areas.
- While each community could make a strong case for retaining, or for the inclusion of, a range of social facilities within their locales, this is not possible in the current economic climate. Furthermore, it is likely that rural communities may face the consolidation of existing services going forward; such as rural schools with low year-on-year enrolments. While a harsh reality, there will need to be an acceptance that not every rural community can be home to all necessary services – for this to be accepted, connectivity to larger rural settlements or neighbouring urban centres will have to be improved – and such realities will have to be built into future 'quality of life' decisions; including whether or not to live in the countryside.

8.3 Role of Spatial Planning and the Micro-Region

Spatial planning policy has a key role to play in promoting sustainability (Taylor, 2008); this includes widening the type and range of development activities permitted in rural areas so that communities do not become over-dependent on single activities / sectors. When planning for rural areas, local councils must achieve a balance between social, economic and environmental development – and in this regard, many councils are proactive and engage in practices that do not preclude development outside of the larger urban centres (which is key to sustainable rural development).

Increasing focus is being placed on the horizontal and vertical integration of planning policy; and linking this integration to the extent to which councils then have access to exchequer funding. At a local level, integrated plans are now being prepared for settlements of various sizes but scope exists to extend this further – so that the more rural and smaller towns and villages are better planned for in terms of their social and economic development. This includes recognising the contribution of asset- and land-based activities to rural economies.

8.3.1 The Micro-Region

In the short-to medium-term, communities must explore and where possible adopt a micro-region perspective to rural restructuring. This can be achieved through a spatial planning approach to development which is fluid, geographically defined with 'fuzzy boundaries' and which can adapt to changing needs. It involves both the physical outcome of development and also the collaboration (partnership; networking; finance) necessary for making this happen. This shift in focus has been brought about by fundamental socio-economic changes such as in communication (road and telecoms) as well as the globalised economy, influencing trade and capital at local, regional, national and international levels.

As communities change their perspective from focusing only on individual villages or townlands – the micro *settlement* – and conceive of the micro-*region* – it will be possible to change from a constant state of competition, both in business and for scarce resources, to cooperation that builds on critical mass, networks and economics of scale.

8.3.2 Developing an Evidence-Base

Future programmes must be evidence-based to monitor performance and impact and provide timely feedback to adjust programmes as they are implemented. Aligning the timing, categories and key questions between the two population censuses for the island of Ireland is a first step.

In addition, the Northern Ireland Census should be carried out more frequently then the current 10-year programme of data-collection. As things stand, the census data for 2001 (the last figures available for Northern Ireland) are of limited use given the extent to which the jurisdiction has changed in the intervening period. Secondly, there is a growing case to be made for an EU-wide census whereby the same questions are asked on the same date in the same year. This would facilitate analysis below the current NUTSIII level and assist in the earmarking of funding to the most appropriate 'micro' locations.

8.3.3 A Changing Policy Landscape

This is an opportune time to be considering the future focus of rural development and restructuring activities. A number of national and regional policy frameworks are being reviewed and where relevant, revised; albeit to varying scales and with differing degrees of public input. Despite this, it is likely that any future rural activities will be guided by the review of the relevant national and regional strategies in both jurisdictions; and more specifically by the *Regional Planning Guidelines* in Ireland and PPS21 in Northern Ireland (although its future is still unclear).

8.3.4 The Review of Public Administration

The planning system structures and processes, North and South, are at variance with each other and this stifles opportunities for cross-border collaboration and the development of integrated frameworks and strategies. It is hoped, however, that the Review of Public Administration (RPA) in Northern Ireland – which will result in a reduction in the number of district councils and the further decentralisation of functions to local government – will make the workings of local government more compatible across the island of Ireland when rolled-out in 2011.

While this review has the potential to secure the long-term viability of rural areas in Northern Ireland and along the Border, it will be necessary for systems to be put in place to ensure that the current fears of rural communities – that sufficient resources, financial and other, will not be directed towards rural settlements (that the new 'super-councils' will be overwhelmed by the commitments needed in urban centres) – are addressed. One such way of doing this is the adoption of the micro-region concept through which a system of integrated planning and resource allocation can be applied; thus responding to the opportunities that can be derived from emphasising the rural-urban interrelationship.

8.3.5 The Rural-Urban Relationship

Towns and villages throughout the island of Ireland have changed significantly in the past twenty years – physically, socially and economically. The process of rural restructuring has involved the renegotiation of place on an on-going basis; part of which has involved a shift from the traditional view of a rural-urban dichotomy to a rural-urban relationship. Under the traditional perspective, rural areas were increasingly dependent on their neighbouring urban centres; with urban governance and policy dictating the role and function of the surrounding peri-urban and rural areas. More recently, technological changes have provided opportunities for rural areas to compete for business investment and EU and national policy have recognised the value of smaller rural settlements working in partnership with larger urban centres. This has entailed increasing emphasis being placed on collaboration through local economic development, the promotion of complimentary functional areas and sustaining rural communities by harnessing their potentiality. However, rural communities will remain dependent on urban-based employment to some extent; at least one member of the household working in higher paid employment in the towns and larger urban centres will play a key role in sustaining the rural economies.

Going forward, development policies for the rural and urban must be increasingly integrated – not only at a planning level but also through enterprise supports, social policies (health, education) – and take cognisance of the micro-region's "spatial and functional interdependencies" (Davoudi & Stead, 2002:273).

8.3.6 Stakeholder Engagement

©IRD Duhallow

Growth secured through managed restructuring will enhance the natural environment and built heritage of rural areas because of the spatial planning approach to development that requires comprehensive stakeholder involvement. Critical to this, of course, is the challenge of meaningful engagement by participants in these processes. The achievement of sustainable rural development in an integrated manner is, according to those who live and work in the three case study areas, closely linked to the roll-out of strategic spatial planning policy. It requires having a shared vision on how the area should develop and clarity of function as well as an acute awareness of the area's 'potentiality'. To translate policy to practice, it is essential to:

- Ensure there is an economic element to the plan for the area (that emphasis is not purely on social development)
- Have a 'champion' who is willing to bring the community together and push hard for action
- Be entrepreneurial and willing to take risks (not being hampered by a lack of resources or finance)
- Recognise the value of the local skills-base and the role of education in (re)training and up-skilling.

These do not simply 'happen' but rather require *inter alia* leaders with the capacity to communicate effectively and demonstrate knowledge and sympathetic – but objective – understanding of the areas, policies and sectors involved.

8.1.7 Recommended Policy & Practice Change

EU Level

- There is a need for greater collaboration between DG Agri and DG Regio within the European Commission so as to realign policies and ensure there is a more balanced allocation of resources between agricultural policies and wider rural development initiatives.

National Level

- Greater emphasis needs to be placed by the relevant government departments and statutory agencies on progressing the various initiatives that are examining the evidence-base that exists across the island of Ireland and the ways in which it can be improved and made more accessible.
- The training of planners (both IPI and RTPI recognised[15]) should include a specific module on rural development; its focus being on what it takes to sustain the rural economy. It is increasingly apparent that rural development is inextricably linked to housing provision in the minds of planners (and others) and this needs to be tackled – as the future of the rural is dependent on much more than this.

Regional Level

- As mooted in the 2009 Irish *Planning and Development (Amendment) Bill*, local planning policies must comply with regional and national policy. Such vertical and horizontal integration will ensure that while development is permitted in the rural, this does not happen to the extent that there is overzoning or oversupply of

15. Training programmes for planners working on the island of Ireland are professionally recognised by the Irish Planning Institute (IPI) and / or the Royal Town Planning Institute (RTPI).

development; that policies for the urban and rural are integrated; and the current leakage of development from larger urban centres, including the designated hubs, is plugged.

Local Government

- Continuing Professional Development (CPD) for local elected officials needs to be introduced to local government. This should cover such issues as EU Directives (such as the Water Framework Directive), planning policy, the 'common good' and what this actually means, and identifying and unleashing local endogenous potential.
- Through the community departments of local government, greater emphasis needs to be placed on encouraging community engagement in policy development at county and regional level. This can be done through the community departments existing links with community networks and forums – rather than placing the emphasis on the individual.

Community Level

- Communities must proactively engage in the preparation of regional guidelines and county development plans. This can happen through community networks and forums (a collective voice); it is therefore important that local development groups engage with, and become members of, such networks.

8.4. Building on Experience: The Last Word to the Case Studies

Reflecting on twenty-plus years of experience, the staff and Board of Directors of both Workspace and IRD Duhallow are in a position to share good practice with other communities challenged by the need for rural restructuring and economic diversification:

- Ensure that the right people are involved from the outset. Those involved should have strong leadership skills, be visionary, entrepreneurial and innovative, and be willing to take risks
- The Board, when established, should be of a limited size, have a clear mandate and be committed to the area in question. It is helpful if members of the Board reside in or have a connection to the area and also have a good network of contacts
- Meet the challenges of the time
- Community buy-in must be secured at the outset and, where possible, this should include newcomers to the area
- Devise a succession plan; this includes building up a volunteer base. This will become increasingly important under the current Cohesion Process whereby Board members must be rotated every three years
- Be original in your thinking and way of working. Because 'no one model fits all', do not lift a model from somewhere else
- Build a certain degree of flexibility into the core objectives. Put in place a plan or framework to which the organisation can work towards and which includes short-, medium- and long-term objectives

- Understand that a development organisation will not be capable of meeting all the social, economic or physical needs of an area, and therefore should not strive to be "all things to all people"
- Know how the funding programmes work and if / how specific programmes can benefit your organisation in meeting its objectives and vision
- If relevant, engage in transnational programmes – but do so only when the organisation has the relevant resources (competencies, time, monies) in place
- Not all programmes of action will be successful. Know when to pull out / end a programme
- Celebrate the successes; share the experience and good news with others. This necessitates having a good communication strategy in place to disseminate results/ findings from projects and programmes
- Outputs are essential; while process is important, it becomes less so if there is no product at the end of the initiative
- Invest in local people. This can be done in a number of ways; for example, through the provision of training, employing local people
- Re-invest in the community. This too can take many forms; the establishment of an after-schools club, the provision of community infrastructure such as a leisure centre.

Self-help is an important aspect of rural restructuring and economic development, working from the bottom-up and focusing on local endogenous potential; but equally *help is also needed* from across the various levels and agencies of government and this must be offered in a coherent, integrated and complementary top-down approach.

References

AEIDL (1999) *Territorial Competitiveness: Creating a territorial development strategy in light of the LEADER experience, Part 1.* Brussels: AEIDL, LEADER European Observatory.

Bartley, B. (2007) 'Planning in Ireland', in Bartley, B. and Kitchin, R. (eds) *Understanding Contemporary Ireland.* London: Pluto, 31-43

Baumgartner, R (2008) 'Managing Innovation in Europe's Cross-Border Micro-Regions'. *Presentation to the 8th EURAM Conference*, 14-17 May 2008. Ljubljana and Bled. Slovenia.

BMW: Border Midlands & Western Regional Assembly (2005) *New Challenges, New Opportunities, Report of the Border, Midland and Western Regional Foresight Exercise, 2005-2025.* Dublin: Brunswick Press Ltd.

Callanan, S et al (2004) *Rural Enterprise Development and Sustainability: Innovative Approaches to the Needs of Rural Areas,* A Literature Review and Survey, NUI Galway and University College Cork, December 2004.

CEC (Commission of the European Communities) (2008) *Working for the Regions: EU Regional Policy 2007-2013,* Luxembourg: Office for the Official Publications of the European Communities.

CEC (2007) *Regions for Economic Change: Fostering competitiveness through innovative technologies, products and healthy communities*, DG Regio, Luxembourg: Office for the Official Publications of the European Communities.

CEC (2006a) *Community strategic guidelines for rural development (programming period 2007 to 2013)*, Council Decision of 20 February 2006, 2006/144/EC. Official Journal L 055, 25/02/2006 P. 0020 – 0029.

CEC (2006b) *EU Directive on the protection of groundwater against pollution and deterioration*, Council Directive 2006/118/EC of 12 December 2006. Luxembourg: Office for the Official Publications of the European Communities.

CEC (2006c) *Conference Proceedings: Regions for Economic Change*, Luxembourg: Office for the Official Publications of the European Communities.

CEC (2003) 'Europe's Rural Areas – An Invaluable Asset for Us All'. *Opening Address by Dr. Franz Fischler, EU Commissioner responsible for Agriculture, Rural Development and Fisheries. Salzburg European Conference on Rural Development*, Salzburg, 13 November 2003.

CEC (2001) *A Sustainable Europe for a Better World: A European Union Strategy for Sustainable Development.* Brussels: European Commission.

CEC (2000) *EU Directive establishing a framework for Community action in the field of water policy*, Council Directive 2000/60/EC of 23 October 2000. Luxembourg: Office for the Official Publications of the European Communities.

CEC (1999) *European Spatial Development Perspective: Towards Balanced and Sustainable Development of the Territory of the European Union.* Luxembourg: Office of the Official Publications of the European Communities.

CEC (1997) *Agenda 2000: For a stronger and wider EU.* Volume 1, Luxembourg: Office for the Official Publications of the European Communities.

CEC (1996) *The Cork Declaration.* The European Conference on Rural Development. Brussels: AEIDL.

CEC (1994) *Europe 2000+: Cooperation for European Territorial Development. Luxembourg:* Office for the Official Publications of the European Communities.

CEC (1993) *Growth, competitiveness, and employment: The challenges and ways forward into the 21st century.* White Paper. Luxembourg: Office of the Official Publications of the European Communities.

CEC (1992) *EU Directive on the conservation of natural habitats and of wild fauna and flora*, Council Directive 92/43/EEC of 21 May 1992. Luxembourg: Office for the Official Publications of the European Communities.

CEC (1988) *The Future of Rural Society.* Luxembourg: Office of the Official Publications of the European Communities

CEC (1979) *EU Directive on the conservation of wild birds*, Council Directive 79/409/EEC of 2 April 1979. Luxembourg: Office for the Official Publications of the European Communities.

Central Statistics Office (2006a): *Census of Population 2006: Volume 1 – Population Classified by Area.* Dublin: The Stationery Office.

Central Statistics Office (2006b): *Census of Population 2006: Volume 7 - Principal Economic Status and Industries.* Dublin: The Stationery Office.

Cloke, P. and Milbourne, P. (1992) Deprivation and Lifestyles in Rural Wales II: rurality and the cultural dimension. *Journal of Rural Studies*, 8(4), 359-371.

Clout, H.D. (1998) The European Countryside: contested space, in Graham, B. (ed) *Modern Europe: place, culture and identity*. London: Arnold

Commins, P. (2004) "Territorial impacts of Common Agricultural Policy, EU Rural Development Policy, Telecom services and Networks and Research and Development" presentation to ESPON (European Spatial Planning Observation Network) seminar *Polycentric Urban Development and Urban – Rural Relations*, NIRSA, NUI Maynooth, May 2004.

Committee of the Regions (COR) (2009) 'Opinion – Think Small First – A Small Business Act for Europe', Comment by Cllr. Constance Hanniffy, COR Commission for Economic and Social Policy. *Regions and Cities of Europe*, No. 63, February-March 2009, 10.

Courtney, P. & Errington, A. (2000) 'The Role of Small Towns in the Local Economy and Some Implications for Development Policy'. *Local Economy*, 15(4), 280-301.

Creamer, C., Blair, N., O'Keeffe, B., Van Egeraat, C. and Driscoll, J. (2008) *Fostering Mutual Benefits in Cross-Border Areas: the challenges and opportunities in connecting Irish border towns and villages.* Armagh, ICLRD.

Crowley, C., Walsh, J., and Meredith, D. (2008) *Irish Farming at the Millennium – A Census Atlas.* NIRSA: Maynooth.

Davoudi, S & Stead, D (2002) 'Rural-urban relationships: An introduction and brief history'. *Built Environment Journal*, 28(4), 269-277.

Department of Agriculture and Food (1999) *Ensuring the Future - A Strategy for Rural Development in Ireland.* Dublin: The Stationery Office.

Department of Agriculture and Rural Development (2006) *Rural Strategy 2007-2013.* Belfast: DARD.

Department of An Taoiseach (2002) *National Spatial Strategy for Ireland 2002-2020: People, Places and Potential.* Dublin: The Stationery Office.

Department of Environment (2009) *Local Government Reform Programme*, see http://www.doeni.gov.uk/index/local_government/local_government_taskforce.htm, accessed 29 May 2009.

Department of the Environment (2008) *Draft Planning Policy Statement 21: Sustainable Development in the Countryside.* Belfast: Corporate Document Services.

Department of the Environment (2007) *Draft Planning Policy Statement 14: Sustainable Development in the Countryside.* Belfast: Corporate Document Services.

Department of the Environment (2003) *Draft Planning Policy Statement 4: Industry, Business and Distribution.* Belfast: Corporate Document Services.

Department of the Environment (1999) *Planning Policy Statement 6: Planning Archaeology and the Built Heritage.* Belfast: Corporate Document Services.

Department of the Environment, Heritage and Local Government (2005) *Sustainable Rural Housing – Guidelines for Planning Authorities.* Dublin: The Stationery Office.

Department of Finance (2006) *National Development Plan 2007-2013, Transforming Ireland: A Better Quality of Life for All.* Dublin: The Stationery Office.

Department for Regional Development (2001) *Shaping our Future - Regional Development Strategy for Northern Ireland, 2025.* Belfast: Corporate Document Services.

Dijkstra, L & Poelman, H (2008) "Remote Rural Regions: How proximity to a city influences the performance of rural regions" in *Regional Focus*, No. 1, European Commission, Brussels.

ESPON: European Spatial Planning Observation Network (2004) *ESPON Project 2.1.3 - The Territorial Impact of CAP and Rural Development Policy, Final Report, August 2004.* Arkleton Institute for Rural Development Research, University of Aberdeen. Luxembourg: ESPON

Garrod, B., Youell, R., & Wornell, R. (2006) 'Re-conceptualising rural resources as countryside capital: The case of rural tourism'. *Journal of Rural Studies*, 22(1), 117-128.

Gleeson, J., Kitchin, R., Bartley, B., Driscoll, J., Foley, R., Fotheringham, A.S. and Lloyd, C. (2007) *The Atlas of the Island of Ireland: Mapping Social and Economic Change.* Maynooth: AIRO

McHugh, C. (2001) *A Spatial Analysis of Socio-economic Adjustments in Rural Ireland 1986-1996*, Thesis submitted for the degree of Ph.D., Faculty of Arts, Department of Geography, National University of Ireland, Maynooth.

IRD Duhallow (2008) *Annual Report.* Newmarket: IRD Duhallow

IRD Duhallow (2004) *Annual Report.* Newmarket: IRD Duhallow

Inter*Trade*Ireland (2006): *Spatial Strategies on the Island of Ireland: Development of a Framework for Collaborative Action*, Prepared by International Centre for Local and Regional Development (ICLRD), May 2006.

Lapping, M.B. (2006) Rural Policy and Planning, in Cloke, P.; Marsden, T. and Mooney, P.H. (eds) *Handbook of Rural Studies.* London: Sage, 104-122

Monaghan County Council (2007) *Monaghan County Development Plan 2007-2013.*

NISRA: Northern Ireland Statistics and Research Agency (2005) *Report of the Inter-Departmental Urban-Rural Definition Group – Statistical Classification and Delineation of Settlements.* February 2005, Belfast: NISRA.

Northern Ireland Assembly (2002) *Gender Inequality in Northern Ireland.* Research Paper 28/02. Research and Library Series. Belfast: Corporate Document Services.

OECD: Organisation for Economic Co-Operation and Development (2009) *A new role for regional policy: local responses for a global crisis.* Closing remarks by Angel Gurría, OECD Secretary-General, delivered at the Ministerial meeting of the territorial development policy committee, Paris, 31 March 2009.

OECD (2006) *Investment Priorities for Rural Development.* Report of conference proceedings, Edinburgh, Scotland, 19-20 October, 2006.

OECD (2005a) *Place-based policies for rural development - Lake Balaton, Hungary (case study)*, Working Party on Territorial Policy in Rural Areas, November 2005. Paris: OECD.

OECD (2005b) *Culture and Local Development.* Paris: OECD.

OECD (2004) *Placed-based policies for rural development - Extremadura, Spain (case study)*, Working Party on Territorial Policy in Rural Areas, December 2004. Paris: OECD.

OECD (2001) *Growth Effects of Education and Social Capital in the OECD Countries. Economic Studies*, No. 33, 2001/II. Paris: OECD.

OECD (1994) *Creating rural indicators for shaping territorial policy.* Paris: OECD.

Pacione, M. (1984) *Rural Geography.* London: Harper and Row

Pearse, J. (2003) *Social Enterprise in Anytown.* London: Calouste Gulbenkian Foundation

Planning and Development (Amendment) Bill 2009. Dublin: The Stationery Office.

Planning and Development Act 2000. Dublin: The Stationery Office.

Planning (Northern Ireland) Order 1991. (N.I.11) Richmond: Office of Public Sector Information

Porter, Michael E. (1998) 'Clusters and the New Economy'. *Harvard Business Review*, 76(6), 77-90. November - December 1998.

PricewaterhouseCoopers (2005) *A Study of Rural Policy.* Study commissioned by DARD (Department of Agriculture and Rural Development). Belfast: Corporate Document Service.

Strategic Investment Board (2008) *Investment Strategy for Northern Ireland 2008-2018: Building a Better Future.* Belfast: SIB Ltd.

Taskforce on Active Citizenship (2007) *Report of the Taskforce on Active Citizenship.* Dublin: The Stationery Office.

Taylor, M (2008) *Living Working Countryside: The Taylor Review of Rural Economy and Affordable Housing*, London: Department for Communities and Local Government.

United Nations Department of Economic and Social Affairs (1992) *Agenda 21*, Division for Sustainable Development. Geneva: UN.

Van der Ploeg, J.D & Renting, H (2000) 'Impact and Potential: A Comparative Review of European Rural Development Practices'. *Sociologia Ruralis*, Vol. 40(4), pp.529-543.

Welsh Assembly Government (2008). *People, Place, Futures – The Wales Spatial Plan*, 2008 Update. Cardiff: The Publications Centre.

Woods, M (2005) *Rural Geography.* London: Sage.

Appendices

APPENDIX 1:

The International Centre for Local and Regional Development

A registered charity based in Armagh, Northern Ireland, the International Centre for Local and Regional Development (ICLRD) is a North-South-US partnership established in 2006 to explore and expand the contribution that planning and the development of physical, social and economic infrastructures can make to improve the lives of people on the island of Ireland and elsewhere. The partner institutions began working together in 2004 and currently include: the National Institute for Regional and Spatial Analysis (NIRSA) at the National University of Ireland, Maynooth; the School of the Built Environment at the University of Ulster; the Institute for International Urban Development in Cambridge, Massachusetts; the Centre for Cross Border Studies in Armagh and the Athlone Institute of Technology.

Each of these partners brings together complementary expertise and networks on both a North-South and East-West basis – creating a unique, all-island and international centre. ICLRD continues to expand its collaboration with other institutions and has built up close working relationships with individual faculty and researchers from Harvard University, Mary Immaculate College Limerick and Queens University Belfast. It is also developing its international linkages, particularly with those organisations that have an interest in cross-border cooperation and collaboration; for example, Mission Opérationnelle Transfrontaliére (MOT) in France.

What does the ICLRD do?

- Provides independent joined-up research and policy advice on cross-border and all-island spatial planning and local and regional development issues (economic development, transport, housing, the environment, service provision)
- Offers capacity building programmes for communities and local, regional and national government representatives and officials
- Assists local governments / communities in translating policy into 'on the ground' action
- Acts as a catalyst to bring relevant public and private actors, North and South, together to work on common goals
- Promotes international cooperation and exchanges.

How does the ICLRD do this?

The ICLRD uses a variety of strategies to undertake its work, including:

- Engaging in action research with local governments, communities and central agencies that contributes to the practical understanding of the complex inter-jurisdictional and cross-border dynamics and drivers of change
- Undertaking case study research to evaluate / develop good practice models
- Hosting workshops on key themes, and the development and delivery of training modules
- Facilitating community groups and local governments in the identification and roll-out of local development initiatives
- Providing sustained strategic cooperation, rather than 'one-off' projects, among academic institutions and the public / private sectors.

In cooperation with the Centre for Cross Border Studies, the ICLRD is starting an exciting new programme to develop a cross-border planning network. This initiative has been made possible through funding from the EU's INTERREG IVA Programme; administered through the Special EU Programmes Body (SEUPB). Commencing in 2009 for three years, the new network (CroSPlaN) will undertake the following activities:

- Two action research projects per year that will enhance emerging cross-border activities and expertise in the vital area of spatial planning
- One executive training programme per year for at least 30 central and local government officials, councillors and community leaders to assist them in both delivering and supporting these activities
- An annual conference and technical workshop; the dual function of which is to facilitate networking and address identified areas of need.

The cross-border planning network, CroSPlaN, will further the integration of transnational, national and local development policies and agendas that combine economic development with concerns for environmental quality, social inclusion and sustainability.

APPENDIX 2:

Interviewee Listing

Draperstown

1. Brian Murray, CEO, Workspace
2. Con Gallagher, Managing Director, Homeseal (Workspace Company)
3. Celine O'Hara, Office Manager, Workspace
4. Margaret Heron, Network Personnel Manager (Workspace Company)
5. Ann McBride, Network Personnel Assistant Manager (Workspace Company)
6. Marion McCloskey, Homeseal General Manager (Workspace Company)
7. Michael Heron, Former Board Member, Workspace
8. Peter Hegarty, Local Businessman
9. Laurence O'Kane, Local Businessman
10. Cllr. Kate Lagan, Magherafelt District Council (and Board of Workspace)
11. Kate Clifford, Rural College & Derrynoid Centre
12. Shane Campbell, Rural College & Derrynoid Centre
13. Chris McCarney, Magherafelt Area Partnership
14. Patsy McShane, Director & Former CEO, Workspace

Emyvale-Truagh-Aughnacloy

15. Fr Sean Nolan, Truagh Development Association
16. Mary Devlin, Truagh Development Association
17. Josie Brady, Truagh Development Association
18. Michael Treanor, Truagh Development Association
19. Fionnuala Cole, Truagh Development Association
20. Eugene McKenna, Truagh Development Association
21. Frank McKenna, Truagh Development Association
22. Marian Dudley, Truagh Development Association
23. Gene Flood, Carrickroe Community Centre
24. Proinsias McKenna, Carrickroe
25. John Joe Connolly, Carrickroe
26. Brian Deary, Carrickroe
27. Maureen Kelly, Emyvale
28. Eamon McMeel, Emyvale
29. Brian McMeel, Emyvale
30. Fiona McConnell, A.W.O.L Paintball & Activity Centre
31. Angela Forde, Mullan
32. Marion Donnelly, Silver Hill Foods, Emyvale
33. Padraig McGeough, Moy Furniture, Emyvale
34. Adrian Corrigan, CNI Monaghan Ltd., Emyvale
35. Jennifer Lambe, Carisma, Aughnacloy
36. Martin Mullen, Carisma, Aughnacloy
37. Gerard Cullen, County Monaghan Partnership
38. Julie-Ann Spence, Blackwater Regional Partnership
39. Catherine Fox, Blackwater Regional Partnership
40. Kellie McAnenly, Moybridge
41. Wayne Morrow, Businessman (Aughnacloy)
42. Liz Salter, Aughnacloy Development Association
43. Breda Meaney, Aughnacloy Development Association
44. Malcolm Duffey, Aughnacloy Development Association
45. Laura Sally, Aughnacloy
46. Eithne McCord, Aughnacloy

47. Niall McKenna, Supervalu, Aughnacloy
48. Eugene O'Hagan, Killybrone
49. Adge King, Monaghan County Development Board
50. Declan Nelson, County Manager, Monaghan County Council
51. Toirleach Gourley, Planning Dept., Monaghan County Council
52. Adrian Hughes, Planning Dept., Monaghan County Council
53. Cllr. Brian McKenna, Emyvale (Monaghan County Council)
54. Vinny Beggs, Enterprise, Investment & Grants Manager, Dungannon & South Tyrone Borough Council

Duhallow

55. Maura Walsh, Manager, IRD Duhallow
56. Michael Doyle, Board Member, IRD Duhallow
57. Thomas Hayes, Kerry County Enterprise Board
58. Donal Murphy, Planning Dept., Kerry County Council
59. John Breen, Kerry County Development Board
60. Breda Mulryan, Area Engineer, Kerry County Council
61. Cllr. Tom Fleming, Scartaglen (Kerry County Council)
62. Rochie Holohan, Cork County Enterprise Board
63. Kevin Lynch, Planning Dept., Cork County Council
64. Sharon Corcoran, Cork County Development Board
65. Tom Stritch, Mallow Town Manager
66. Jack Roche, Board Member, IRD Duhallow
67. Noel Dillon, Board Member, IRD Duhallow
68. John Moynihan, Board Member, IRD Duhallow
69. Cormac Collins, Board Member, IRD Duhallow
70. Don Crowley, Board Member, IRD Duhallow
71. Billy Murphy, Board Member, IRD Duhallow
72. Helen O'Sullivan, IRD Duhallow
73. Eileen Linehan, IRD Duhallow
74. Catherine Crowley, IRD Duhallow
75. Colm Crowley, IRD Duhallow

National / Regional

76. Michael Hughes, Director, Rural Community Network
77. Eoin Magennis, Policy Research Manager, InterTradeIreland
78. Jim Hetherington, Department for Regional Development
79. Niall Cussen, Department of the Environment, Heritage and Local Government
80. Michael O'Corcora, Department of Community, Rural & Gaeltacht Affairs
81. Susan Scally, Department of Community, Rural & Gaeltacht Affairs
82. Dairearca Ni Neill, Department of Community, Rural & Gaeltacht Affairs
83. Padraig Maguire, Border Regional Authority
84. Paul Donnelly, Department of Agriculture and Rural Development
85. Shane McKinney, Department of Agriculture and Rural Development
86. Gerard Tracey, Department of Agriculture and Rural Development